Druidry

The Ultimate Guide to the Way of the Druids and What You Should Know About Herbs, Ogham, Rituals, Divination, Druid Tarot Reading, and Runes

Your Free Gift (only available for a limited time)

Thanks for getting this book! If you want to learn more about various spirituality topics, then join Mari Silva's community and get a free guided meditation MP3 for awakening your third eye. This guided meditation mp3 is designed to open and strengthen ones third eye so you can experience a higher state of consciousness. Simply visit the link below the image to get started.

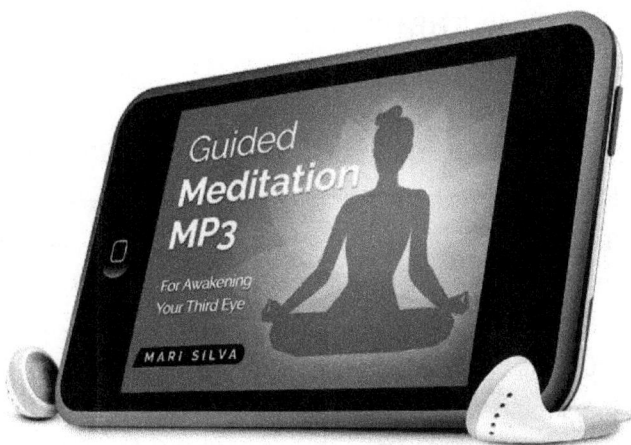

https://spiritualityspot.com/meditation

Contents

Introduction

Do you spend your life just getting through each day in a daze? As you trudge through each day, are you doing the same things the same way every time? Or do you ever stop and think – there must be more to life than this?

Well, there is always a different, better way to live your life, and that way is Druidry. What on earth is that, you ask? Aren't Druids religious fanatics who worship at Stonehenge, wearing strange clothing? How can that possibly help you change your life?

Druidry has nothing to do with any of that. Druidry is a way of life based on an understanding and appreciation of nature and all things natural, but you don't have to live in the countryside or the middle of nowhere to practice this lifestyle. This book will teach you everything you need to know about Druidry without you having to follow any religious beliefs, ideals, or perceptions.

The sheer beauty of Druidry lies in the fact that you can follow it any way you please. There is no need to follow a set of rules when you can follow your own and achieve the same. How you worship your deity and frame your deity's concept is entirely up to you.

So, what makes this book different from all the other books on Druidry? Well, this one contains the most up-to-date information and is presented in an easy-to-read manner. Each topic follows the last one seamlessly, and it is entirely suitable for those who want to brush up their knowledge on Druidry and those who know nothing about it but want to learn.

Inside you will find clear information and plenty of hands-on rites and rituals you can do yourself. You will also find prayers you can recite, even adding your own words, and lots of different tarot spreads to learn and understand.

Everything you ever needed to know about Druidry is contained in these pages, and by the end of the book, you will be ready to start living life the way you deserve to.

Chapter 1: Who Are the Druids?

The druids have to be one of the most enigmatic groups in history. These days, there are two primary neo-druid sects, and they both focus their philosophy on love, diversity, and nature. They are the people you are likely to see cloaked and performing ceremonies at Stonehenge and other megalithic sites.

The Ancient druids are shrouded in the mists of folklore and legend, and no written records detail who they were and where they originated. If you believe the consensus, then they were a revered group of people with wisdom far beyond the highest of nobilities and a divine connection to all things nature. They are thought to be Celtic, but other theories claim they share a common ancestry with the ancient East.

The Ancient Druids

We can describe druidism as a shamanic religion, mostly because it relies on holistic medicines (for both treating and causing illnesses) combined with contacting the spirit world. Sometimes, Druids were said to have brought about insanity in people and were also touted as accurate fortunetellers.

The history that surrounds the druids is shrouded in mystery, mostly because of limited record. It was thought that druidism was part of the European Gaulish and Celtic cultures, and the first classical reference can be dated to the second century BC.

Druid practices are comparable to how today's priests create a connection between people and the Gods. Their role was somewhat more varied, as they were scientists, teachers, philosophers, and judges. They were respected and powerful, with the ability to banish a person from society if they broke one or more of the sacred laws. They even had the power to broker peace between opposing armies. They never paid taxes; they never served in battle, and for the most part, druid women were equal to druid men, which was somewhat unusual for ancient communities. Women could divorce their husbands and participate in battles and wars.

We can date an early account of the druids back to 59-51 BC. Julius Caesar wrote it in Gaul, a place where the most prestigious men were divided into two - noble and druids. A vast amount of knowledge we have about druids is thanks to the Roman writers. Like the Romans and the Greeks, the druids were polytheistic, worshipping female sacred figures and goddesses. Because they were not so civilized and were nomadic, they gained a sense of superiority. That means many accounts we do have can't be taken as historically factual as they may include details of exaggerations in terms of druid practices. We know there are recordings of human sacrifices by the druids, but we have no evidence to support it.

It is believed that the druid class was divided into subsections, each with its own color-coded robes. The wisest eldest druid was known as the Arch-druid, and his robes were gold. Ordinary druids would wear white robes and be the priests, while Sacrificers would wear red robes and fighters. The blue-robed druids were the artistic ones, and new recruits would wear black or brown robes, be issued with lower-ranked tasks, and not held in high esteem.

Every aspect of druidism was ordered and structured, from the class hierarchy to their life patterns in tune with nature's cycles. They observed the seasonal, solar, and lunar cycles, and their worship was according to those cycles on eight holy days.

I will go into more detail about this later, but druids celebrated the New Year on Hallowe'en (Samhain) because this was the day of the last harvest. Samhain is a day of spirituality and mysticism because it was when the living and the dead were the closest they will ever be too revealing themselves to one another.

The winter solstice is Yule, when druids would seat themselves on earth mounds through the night and wait for sunrise, the time when they believed they would be reborn.

February 2nd is Imbolc, when they celebrate motherhood using sheep's milk. The spring equinox was Ostara, and on April 30th, it was Beltane, the festival of fertility. The summer solstice was Litha, when the druids believed the Holly King took over from the Yule Oak King. The first harvest took place on August 2nd, Lughnasa, and the autumnal equinox was Mabon. The holy day cycle would then start over, repeating itself and reflecting on the cycles of the planets, nature, and life, and druids were firmly in the belief that reincarnation was real. They also believed that if you sinned in one life, you could atone for it in the next.

The Druids' Temples, the places where they worshiped, were secluded and quiet areas, typically clearings in the forests and in stone circles. Stonehenge has to be the most famous of these stone circles, not just in the United Kingdom, but also in the world. Stonehenge dates to around 2400 BC and is one of the most ancient megalithic monuments. When they hear of druids, most people automatically think of them as casting incantations and rituals at the circle of stones. It was thought that Stonehenge was a place of worship for the druids and still is today, for neo-druids and pagans. There is disagreement whether the druids built Stonehenge. We cannot be certain when the druids first arrived in Britain, but probably it was after Stonehenge had been built.

Other druidic sites are believed to be Anglesey, Wistman's Wood (Dartmoor), and the Isle of Ynys Mon. Anglesey was thought to be where the druids were taught – it took around 20 years to learn druidic lore thoroughly and had to be learned by heart – the druids rarely, if ever, used written language, and that is why we don't know that much about them. Gaulish language was limited, originally consisting of Greek letters. When Caesar came to rule, that was changed to Latin, and the old records were eventually lost.

Druids faced Roman oppression in the 1st century AD, and Tiberius even banned druidism altogether, citing the apparent human sacrifices as the reason. In the 2nd century, druidism appeared to disappear altogether, and some theories attempt to explain this. The first theory says that the reason is something that affected many ancient cultures and societies, warfare, famine, and disease, and this could have resulted in the society being wiped out. The second revolves around Christianity and asks whether druids could have been converted. A druid revival occurred in England in Wales in the 1700s with a famous arch-druid, William Blake, participating.

Today, religions like Wicca and Christianity are influenced by druidism – take the number three, for example. Considered significant by the druids, it is also significant for Wiccans and Christians. The Triskele was a symbol made up of three lines that combined to make a circle, and circles were a key part of druid life – the circle of light and darkness, the circle of the seasons, and the circle of life.

To conclude this section, it might even surprise you to learn that Winston Churchill was a druid – although there is no proof of that!

The Modern Druids

Today, Druidry offers one simple beauty - each seeker on the druid path should find his or her own "Truth Against the World." That means that, rather than following a set of standards and rules, druids are encouraged to develop their standards of ethics, practice, and beliefs as they travel the path. Not every modern druid will share the same beliefs, but they are considered an excellent place to start for new druids. As you progress, you may find those beliefs hold true for you, or you may use them as a framework for building your own beliefs and ideas - it is down to you.

One of the most time-honored traditions of passing knowledge to others is answering questions, which I will do for the remainder of this section.

How Does Modern Druidry Compare to Ancient Druidry?

The two are as different as day and night, and that is almost wholly because there are no written records from the ancient druids. We have only legend to base our theories on today, except for writings from those who observed the druids. Though, many of these are too biased to be accepted as believed. There is some history we have learned over the years from the archeological evidence.

Modern Druidry evolved over the years from fantastical 19th-century revivalist stories to today's modern practitioners who have free and easy access to a whole heap of information. Today, druids want to see proof of things, they want a spirituality focused on a hearth or Celtic culture, and they want their own identity. While most want to be authentic, we don't have enough information to make that happen, but not everyone is focused on the scholastic side - they are happy to do what feels right to them.

By today's standards, some of what we can read about the druids, written by the Romans, is illegal, such as human sacrifices. But the Romans were the only ones who ever mentioned it, so we have to question whether it happened or not. Were they sacrificed, or were these humans murdered? Or did the druids sentence criminals to execution? That is something we will never know, but what we do know is that the Celts were known for keeping battle trophies - the heads of the more valiant of their enemies. That too could be questioned - was it a human sacrifice, or merely a way of reaping the rewards of war?

Regardless, we could go on forever, but it remains a fact that human and animal sacrifices are no longer done, nor are they condoned. The same applies to other practices considered illegal, such as wielding bladed weapons improperly in public or taking illegal substances. Again, they may (or may not) have been part of Ancient Druidry but are not condoned by modern druids.

What has been written about the ancient druids does show they were connected to their time. They had dealings with world-wide cultures, had trade agreements, got involved in politics, and used far more advanced healing techniques than the Romans. They also served their communities as teachers, lawyers, lawmakers, ritual leaders, counselors, and spiritual services.

Ancient druids were also well known as educated people. If we could compare what the ancient druids practiced and knew with what modern druids would need to do the same today, they would need college degrees in medicine, law, psychology, religious studies, and education. They would need to be trained in diplomacy, public relations, and know multiple languages. These are the reasons it took over 20 years to become a fully trained druid.

Ancient Druidry was definitely a faith or philosophy in tune with the times, so it makes sense that modern druids follow the same, staying connected with modern times but not losing the connection to our ancient ancestors. Today, we all have our own needs, skills, and cultures, all different from what the ancient druids had, but that must not stop a modern druid from learning Celtic history, researching Celtic culture, and discovering how it has evolved and developed.

Take the Earth, for example. In ancient times, pollution was not considered an issue; today, it is. Every day, our ancient ancestors dealt with survival, with growing and finding food. Today, many of us take supermarkets for granted as a source of food. Many of us neither grow our own nor do we raise animals for meat and other goods. That means we have no real idea of how important the agricultural seasons are and the cost of just trying to survive each day.

Today, druids can still serve their communities by choosing careers that let them serve in a helpful way or by doing community service. Lots of druids train to become lawyers, teachers, psychologists, doctors, engineers, and more. In ancient times, being a druid meant living with and serving society, which is how modern Druidry should be.

Holy Books and Writings Used by Druids

If you think of the Torah used in Judaism or the Bible in Christianity, there are no official holy druid books. And there is a good reason for that. The primary tenet of modern druidism is to seek your own "truth against the world," and a holy book would do nothing more than invalidate that tenet.

What you do have are texts with useful information, and to learn more about the values, leadership, and laws from translated writings, check these out:

• **Audacht Morainn** – Otherwise known as the Testament of Morann, it is a statement detailing the ethics to be followed by a ruler.

• **Cormac's Instructions** – These were instructions from Cormac to his grandson on the virtues that go with good kingship. Translated by Kuno Meyer, you can find them at: http://www.ancienttexts.org/library/celtic/ctexts/cormac3.html

- **Fenechas or Brehon Laws** - More commonly known as the Laws of the Freemen, they come from the Senchus Mor. You cannot get these in their original format any longer, but you can get more information about them from websites and books.

- **The Celtic Triads** - Contains the trials of wisdom passed down through the ages. John F. Wright of Clannada collected many of them, and to date, they have been circulated thousands of times on the Internet with no credit going to him. Although the website is not very well designed, it does give full credit, and you can find all the triads at http://wolf.mind.net/library/celtic/triads/triads.htm

- **The Myths and Legends** - Search the Internet and the libraries, and you will find plenty of information on mythology, depending on the particular hearth culture you follow. If you are looking for the Welsh legends, try the Mabinogion.

If you read a book called the 21 Lessons of Merlynn, written by Douglas Monroe, and a somewhat controversial book you will come across is something called the Book of Pheryllt.

The Barddas is an even older forgery. Claimed as ancient, the Barddas was invented and subsequently written by Edward Williams (Iolo Morganwg) in the 19th century. Reading about what was practiced and believed during the Druid revival makes for good reading - it might not be truthful about druid practice, but it is a part of history modern druids should know.

Most druids prefer to read books properly and thoroughly researched and are well written. There are far too many books that claim they are about Druidry but are nothing more than a poorly written mixture of Pagan or occult philosophies that might have a little Celtic flavor to them.

Those who follow Druidry as a philosophy will likely follow a religion of their own but add a druidic approach to it by adding druidic philosophy. To be fair, the modern druid can be Wiccan, Buddhist, Christian, and many others, and that is the point of modern Druidry – to be yourself but follow the druidic philosophy.

Chapter 2: Are You Ready to Become a Modern Druid?

"Today, far from Druidry seeming like some arcane fringe activity, its preoccupations are now center-stage. They address the most urgent and important issue of our time: how we galvanize all of our potential - practical, creative, intellectual, and spiritual - to protect and restore the Earth.

They address directly the gaze of Greta Thunberg and her generation - our children and grand-children - to say: we are committed to our love of Nature to the fullest extent, with all of our being - all looking towards the same horizon: a world in which every human being has enough to lead a happy, healthy and fulfilling life without suffering injustice, without terrible inequalities between rich and poor, without the destruction of habitats and species, without the pollution of our skies and seas." Philip Carr-Gomm

The Order of Bards, Ovates, and Druids work spiritually and practically with Druidry to address humankind's three biggest yearnings - creativity in our lives, deep communing with nature, and the ability to access great stores of wisdom. Each comes from a different self-aspect, identified in Druidry as The Singer, The Shaman, and The Sage. Bardic teachings aim to nurture The Singer -

the creative part of us, the storyteller, or the artist. Ovate teachings aim to nurture The Shaman, the nature lover and healer, which lies within all of us, and Druid teachings aim to develop our wisdom, also known as The Sage, that lives in all of us.

Typically, Druidry manifests in three ways, all separate from one another:

- **Culturally** - to foster the Breton, Cornish and Welsh languages
- **Fraternally** - to support and raise money for good causes
- **Spiritually** - to help us get in touch with our inner selves

Each approach is based on inspiration from the ancient Druids, the guardians of a religious and wholly magical tradition in existence long before Christianity. Druid influence can be traced from West Irish shores to Western France and way beyond. According to Caesar, Druidry started life in the United Kingdom.

In the 7th century, Christianity replaced Druidry. Although we know little about these Sages, the early 18th century saw groups (who took inspiration from them) form in parts of Britain. Druidry suddenly began to be revived, thanks to British, French, and German scholars who were gripped by the subject, and today, that practice is continued in ever-growing numbers of people inspired by the rituals, teaching, and traditions that have rapidly evolved over the last 200 years.

In particular, modern Druidry seems to appeal to those who no longer see any benefit in traditional and conventional religion and those who seek a deeper spiritual connection to the earth and their ancestors. Today, with the world-changing fast and evolving in an environment under threat, these people seek their roots in Place and Time, seeking reverence for the planet on which we live.

How to Practice Modern Druidry

How you practice modern Druidry is up to you – each practitioner chooses their own way. There is no set-in-stone way; there are as many ways of practicing as there are druids!

There are common things that most modern druids agree on:

• **Truth** – Virtually all modern druids believe that integrity is vital in their everyday lives, alongside searching for Truth. Today, many druids use their studies to seek their own Truth by learning from others' teachings, researching for themselves, using meditation, communing with nature, and carrying out ritual practice to know and understand the Kindreds.

• **Polytheism** – Most neo-pagan druids are polytheistic, believing or worshipping in several deities that usually fall into the same pantheon – all Welsh, all Irish, etc. Celtic Pantheons are the most followed by druids, but ADF druids follow Indo-European Pantheons, such as Germanic, Russian, Norse, and so on. What most druids do agree on is that we shouldn't use a deity for a specific purpose. Wiccans call on deities from multiple pantheons, so long as the deity is suitable for the purpose the correspondence chart states. Many pagans subscribe to a "deity of the week," but many druids do not. Where pagans see individual deities as being part of a specific God or Goddess, Druids tend to see each as an individual, one that must be respected as an individual.

Some Christian druids believe in a single Deity while others don't believe in any, seeing it as nothing more than a philosophy. Neo-pagan druids believe in polytheism.

- **Druids are Welcoming** – Druid rituals are left open for all to attend, and there are no limits on who can train to be a druid. Some neo-pagan groups are a little more exclusive with their teachings and ritual practices and prefer to know a person better before allowing them access to rituals.

- **Magical Workings** – Including spells. While many druids do practice this, it is not their primary focus, and it is not practiced the way Wiccans and other traditions do it. Wiccans hone their skills by practicing magic because that is one of their primary focuses. If a modern druid went through their whole life without ever casting a spell, they would not be thought any less because it is not considered a requirement of Druidry.

- **Nature is Critical** – Most druids revere nature, trying their best to remain aware of their practices, ecologically speaking.

- **They Celebrate a Minimum of Four Holy Days** – Most pagans celebrate eight seasonal festivals – Samhain, Yule (Winter Solstice), Imbolc, Ostara (Spring Equinox), Beltane, Litha (Summer Solstice), Lammas (Lughnassadh), and Macon (Autumn Equinox). However, just four of these are Celtic holidays – Samhain, Beltane, Imbolc, and Lammas. Some druids celebrate all eight holidays while others celebrate just the Celtic holidays, but, typically, unless they belong to a group requiring all the dates to be celebrated, it is down to each individual druid.

- **Service** – Some modern druids seek to serve their community, their needs, and their Gods through ecological awareness, community service, retaining balance in their lives, and maintaining a spiritual practice.

Many see Druidry as a philosophy, using a druidic approach to follow their chosen religions – that approach is druid philosophy.

The Druid Gods and Goddesses

These days, we like to put everything in its place, all in neat little boxes. The Greek Gods go in one box, the Chinese in another, and the Norse go in yet another box. In ancient times, things were not quite so neat. The Anatolians worshiped Akta, a Goddess much admired by the Greeks, so they also named her *Hecate.* The Romans thought so much of Hecate they even erected temples in her name in Rome.

As the Roman Empire spread, temples to Hecate sprang up across the world, but some centuries down the line, British bishops were not happy that the "peasants" worshiped Hecate. Today, she is worshiped worldwide – Athens, London, Sydney, Paris, and so on. She is known as a Greek Goddess, but she was worshipped long before the Greeks even heard her name. Today, nationalities across the world worship her. So, how can she be said to be an exclusively Greek Goddess? And how can any deity be said to be exclusive to one nationality?

In terms of Celtic Gods, we mean those worshipped by the Irish, British, or other Iron Age continental tribes. We should remember that these deities were also popular in other regions too. Nehalennia was a Goddess worshipped by the Celts in what later became Holland, but Germanic tribes and Roman tribes began making offerings to her. These days, people who have no Celtic background at all perform rituals honoring Celtic deities.

Celtic lands are littered with altar stones and statues, many of which are not named – your guess is as good as mine as to whom they represent! Some altars have had names carved into them, and several names appear more frequently than others, while a few show up just once. Some Gods were given different names, so we can't always be sure that a dozen altars are for a dozen different Gods or to one God with a dozen different names.

We need to stop and think about the way the early Irish and British viewed their Gods, whether we share those views or not. These days, Pagans believe that every Goddess is an aspect of One Goddess, and every God is an aspect of One God. This is usually known in academic circles as *duolatry* or *duotheism.* There is nothing wrong with this, but be aware there is little to no evidence that ancient British tribes believed it. Instead, there is an indication they were polytheists, meaning they believed in multiple spirits, Gods, and Goddesses. Each of these was separate and real, not aspects of anything else. You might think that has no bearing, but it does affect how people relate to their Gods.

If druids believe that every God is separate and that every God is unique, they have to relate to each one differently. If, for example, you get on with Danu, it doesn't necessarily mean that you would relate in the same way with An Chailleach. It also follows that not every God relates well to others. After all, when you mix chemicals, you get a damp squib, but others react violently to one another – if Gods attended the same rituals, there could be more than just fireworks!

The ancient druids put little stock in the notions of evil and good. Instead, their moral code was strong, but they didn't think the way modern people do. The Gods are not good, nor are they evil. They just are. If a vicious storm sprung up and your house was struck by lightning, you couldn't say that the lightning was evil; it just does what its nature dictates. Similarly, the Lord of the Dead, Donn, doesn't lead death into our word because he is a cruel master. Death is a natural part of life's cycle – we may not like it, but it happens.

In the same way, polytheists must also learn that while deities may share commonalities, it doesn't make them the same deity, and it doesn't make them identical in any other respect. Rhys and Owen may have the same hair color, but it doesn't follow that they like the same food or read the same books. Moccus and Nuada are warlike, but they have nothing else in common.

We should also remember that Gods are certainly not all-powerful. They have limits. They have to work within the same laws of the universe we all do. That said, Gods are way more powerful than mere mortals. And for that, they deserve a lot of respect. When druids perform rituals, they are not summoning Gods. The Gods do not need invites to attend a ritual. If they want to be there, they will be, whether you like it or not. If they don't want to be there, it won't matter how much you chant, how many candles you light and dance around - they won't show up.

When you encounter the Gods, notice that they each have individual temperaments and characters, shaping how they respond to your requests. This will influence the direction you turn to for help. Many books still say that the God of Thunder is Zeus; the God of the Sun is Apollo, and so on. To a certain point, there is nothing wrong with that, but after a while, it gets somewhat limiting. All Gods have their own interests; they are more than one dimensional in the same way that humans are. When druids think about the deity they want to approach, they don't choose by looking in a book for which God or Goddess deals with that issue.

Let's say you wanted help in finding new employment. If you spoke to a teacher, they would likely tell you the best qualifications you needed to get the job you are after. A model would tell you what kind of clothes you should wear to the interview, while a job center employee would help you write your CV. While each would have input on you getting that job, each way would be different. The person whose help you chose would depend entirely on what you think is effective. Gods work the same way - all can help, but they all have different ways of going about things.

You don't have to be a polytheist to learn about druid ideas and Celtic myths, but knowing how a polytheist thinks will help you understand why rituals are done the way they are.

Most of us know the Old Gods by the names they were given during the Medieval and Dark Age periods when the monks wrote their names. During the Iron Age, they would have been spoken in a different way. Some names come from altar inscriptions, and linguists *guess* how the Gods would have been named before Christianity.

You can see examples of this below:

MEDIEVAL VERSION	IRON AGE VERSION
Lugh	Lugos
Rhiannon/Morrighan	Rigantona
Fionn/Gwynn	Vindos/Vindonnus
Aognhus	Oinogustus
Beli	Belinus
Ogma	Ogmios
Boannan	Bouvinda
Nuada	Nodens
Goibniu	Gobanos
Brigit	Brigantia
Bran	Brannos

In early Celt times, Gods were seen as ancestors, and the Celts often claimed that they descended from one God or another. In essence, they were family, a member of the Tribe. Most likely, people saw them in the way they might have seen a powerful, wise uncle, cousin, father, or mother. And this is reflected in the names the Gods have; for example, An Chailleach could mean The Grandmother.

The deity names below come from inscriptions on altars, statues, and so on from the Romano-British period. Before that, as far as we know, native tribes didn't inscribe the names, so we must remember that these names are often pronunciation attempts of local words by the Romans. As such, these names are not always the same as those used by the natives. And there are likely many more Gods whose inscriptions have not been found. We also don't know how many of these names are merely different names for one God or Goddess.

- **Andraste** – The Goddess of Victory, whom Boudica called on during the rebellion, and who let a hare go to see what course the battle would take.

- **Antenociticus** – This God's name was found near Newcastle-Upon-Tyne, on a small shrine near Benwell. The God is depicted as young with the bud of new antlers upon his head.

- **Arnemetia** – This is more than likely one of Nemetona's titles and was found near a healing spa at Buxton. Nemetona's shrine was found at a spa in Bath.

- **Belatucadros** – A God of war and destruction with a name that translates as "fair shining one." The Romans equated him with God Mars, and other variants of the spelling include Belatucader.

- **Belinus** – The God of light, often called "The Shining One." He oversees sheep and cattle welfare, and his wife is the Goddess names Belisama. Both have been compared to Minerva and Apollo.

- **Belisama** – The Goddess of light and fire, and the Goddess of the forge and crafts. She's Belinus's wife and is also associated with healing springs.

- **Brigantia** – The Goddess of victory, her name is known from British inscriptions. Her name translates to "The Exalted One," and she is often thought to be a guardian deity of the Brigantes. Brigantia is equated with another Goddess named Victoria. She is often depicted with winds, a mural crown, a spear, and a child and has an association with Minerva. The God Bregans was her consort.

- **Callirius** – Callirius has an association with the Roman Woodland God, Silvanus. His name was found on a shrine in Colchester and is associated with the hazel tree. A stag icon was located in the pit.

- **Camulus** – A Celtic warrior God, Camulus was known in Gaul and Britain and was considered important before Roman times. He was equated with Mars, known as Mars Camulos, and gave his name to Camulodunum, otherwise known as Colchester.

- **Cernunnos** – The God of fertility, wild animals, regeneration, and abundance, Cernunnos translates as "antlered one." Images show he (or someone like him) was worshipped across Britain and Gaul, and although his name does not show on any statues in Britain, the images are pretty identical to him.

- **Cocidius** – Known as "The Red One," Cocidius was worshipped mostly near Hadrian's Wall and in Western and Northern Cumbria. He is a God of hunting and woodland and is also a God of War, sometimes seen with a spear and a shield. An inscription was found at Ebchester to Cocidius Vernostonus, and the "vern" indicates "alder tree." Cocidius has, at times, been syncretized with Mars and with Silvanus, and a sanctuary to the God is thought to have been located close to the Irthing River valley.

- **Corotiacus** – He is the God of battle. A depiction of him has been found near Martlesham in Suffolk, showing a man wielding a pair of axes and riding a horse.

- **Coventina** – The Goddess of healing springs at Carrawburgh, close to Hadrian's Wall, is called both "Augusta" and "Sancta" in inscriptions. Typically, she is portrayed as a naked maiden resting on the waves, holding a water lily. One shows her as three different forms, each pouring water out of a jug.

• **Cunomaglus** – The Great Hound or the Great Wolf, the Romans associated Cunomaglus with Apollo, in his healing capacity, his solar capacity, or both.

• **Deae Matres** – Typically seen as a trinity, Deae Matres is often depicted with baskets containing bread, fruit, or fish. She is linked with the sacred springs and statuaries located in London, Lincoln, Bath, and Cirencester.

• **Dea Nutrix** – Otherwise known as the "Nursing Mother, " clay figures show her in a wicker chair with a high back, nursing one or more infants.

• **Epona** – The Horse Goddess, her worship was empire-wide, and December 18th even became a Roman feast-day in her honor.   Depictions of Epona were always of her riding a horse or alongside one, and sometimes she would have a dog, a goose, a key, baskets of fruit, ears of corn, or a plate full of corn.

• **Maponos** – The name translates as "The Young Sun," and inscriptions have been found at Chesterholm and Hadrian's Wall. Typically, he is connected to the Great Mother, Matrona.

• **Mogons** – Translated as "The Great One," we often see his name spelled as Mogonus. Dedications occur around Hadrian's Wall, usually at forts such as Vindolanda, Netherby, Old Penrith, and Risingham, and these are often paired with Apollo.

• **Nemetona** – The Guardian of Sacred Places, a statue of Nemetona, was in Bath, and she was also worshipped across Germany.

- **Nodens** – The God of Healing Sanctuaries, Nodens is associated with hunting and dogs. Temples have been found associated with him at Lydney Park, and these also show sea images, which suggests that Nodens has a link to the ocean.

- **Rosmerta** - This Goddess has been in Germany, Britain, and Gaul as Mercury's companion, and she has also been depicted in the Gloucester Museum on a relief. The relief shows her over an altar, holding a plate.

- **Sulis** – Otherwise known as Bath's patron deity or Aquae Sulis, Sulis is associated with healing, hot springs, and water. The Bath temple has a dedication to Sulis Minerva.

- **Taranis** – The God of thunder and lightning, a wheel symbolizes Taranis. He is archaeologically known in Germany, and Gaul and Lucan mentioned him in Pharsalia. An altar in Chester shows him as linked to Jupiter.

- **Teutates** – Located mainly in Gaul, but an inscription was in Cumberland. His name indicates he is the tribes' patron and protector.

- **Veteris** – Also seen as Vitiris, he is a warrior God, and 54 inscriptions show seven or more versions of his name. Most of these inscriptions were found on the eastern Hadrian's Wall, and some altars show carvings of snakes and boars.

- **Vindonnus** – Very few inscriptions have been located, but those that have been found are in Gaul. Linguists have linked Vindonnus to Fionn and Gwynn. There is a suggestion those figures' roots are in Vindos (a similarly named deity) or in Vindonnus.

From looking at that list, it's clear that you could spend your whole life practicing rituals and never even begin to understand who all these Gods and Goddesses are. Most practicing druids are drawn to a few deities, usually those that they have an affinity with. Some find that a deity will reveal itself when the time is right for a lesson to be taught about life, a part of life they don't have an affinity with at the time.

Let's look at a few of the Gods in close detail.

Ogmios

He is the patron of some Druidry groups. Patrons are known as Flaiths in Gaelic and are a person or deity who watches over you in exchange for support or a few offerings. A Greek writer named Lucian saw Ogmios in Gaul and described him as an older bald man with thin gold chains running from his tongue to the ears of several smiling followers. Though, early Celts never saw their Gods having a human appearance. They saw them as animals and as the forces of nature.

Irish myth tells us of Ogma, a name associated with Ogmios. Ogma is thought to have been the Ogham alphabet's inventor and is described as a poet and a bard. He was given an important title – "The Honey-Tongued" – a title important for those who see language as a vital part of their life.

He had another name – Grianianech, which means Sun-Faced, and also Threnfher, which means Champion. He was considered a sunny presence and a God that loves teaching, learning, and language.

Lugus

The name Lugus shows up in several places in Europe and Britain. He had an Irish form, Lugh, described in Irish myth as having a Tuatha father and a Fomori mother. His name translates as "light," and druids often compare him to the Sun's radiance because he spreads from the east across the land much like the Sun.

One story claims he turned up in Tara at the Tuatha Fortress gates, asking to be let in. When he was asked what skills he possessed, he listed all his talents, but he was told that another God had already taken his skill each time. Finally, he asked them if they had a God who could do all the skills – they didn't, and he was admitted to Tara, bestowing the title of Samildanach on him. That title translates to "many-skilled one," and he led the Tuathan armies in battle against the Fomorian forces. After they were vanquished, he taught a lot of skills during peacetime. He had two very popular gifts for humanity – fidchell (a board game) and horse racing. The Welsh know him as Lleu, and they tell a story about a magical woman he married, a woman made of flowers.

Brigantia

Brigantia had the honor of having a tribe named after her. The tribe owned territories that covered what is now known as Yorkshire. We still see Brigantia, the War-Goddess, depicted on 50 pence coins in the United Kingdom, only we know her as Britannia, her Roman name. The Scots and the Irish knew her as Brighid. She was also considered the Ban-Flaith or female patron of the Leinster province.

When a nun with the same name set a monastery up where a pagan temple once stood, stories about her began to entwine with Goddess's. Eventually, the Abbess Brigit became a Saint, but meanwhile, she maintained a sacred fire in a grove, an old pagan tradition, and only women could go into the grove. Not even the bishop was allowed in!

Fire is essential to Brigantia, especially as she is also the patron of poets, healers, and blacksmiths. She is the guardian of farm beasts, sheep in particular, and one of the most popular pastimes on Brigantia's feast day was to leave bowls of milk out for her animals. Domestic chores commonly associated with Iron Age women in Ireland were churning milk into butter, weaving, spinning, cooking, and creating a good home, and these also came under Brighid's aegis.

These are just three of the more commonly known deities, only the tip of the iceberg, but they do give you something to think about.

The Druid Prayer

Prayer is an essential part of Druidry, be it a solo prayer or a Grove prayer. The following is commonly known as "The Druid's Prayer." It was written and first publicly spoken by Iolo Morganwg in 1792 at the Summer Solstice.

Grant, O God/dess/Spirit/etc., thy protection,

and in protection, strength,

and in strength, understanding,

and in understanding, knowledge,

and in knowledge, the knowledge of justice,

and in the knowledge of justice, the love of it,

and in that love, the love of all existences,

and in the love of all existences, the love of God/dess/etc.,

and all goodness.

Because Druidry allows you to choose your own Gods and your own way in life, it is acceptable to change this prayer's words to suit your circumstances.

Chapter 3: Druid Festivals and Ceremonies

Most Pagans celebrate the wheel of the year calendar, consisting of eight festivals. These are all spaced evenly throughout the year, roughly every six to seven weeks, and four are Celtic with Celtic names. Those who attend these festivals will find that certain rites are practiced, rites that help followers get themselves in tune with the natural life-force rhythms that the seasonal quarters and moon phases mark.

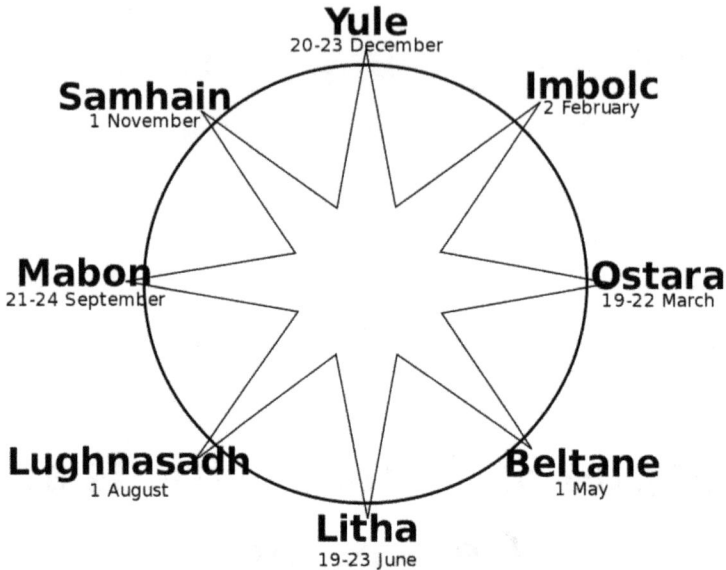

Yule
20-23 December

Imbolc
2 February

Samhain
1 November

Mabon
21-24 September

Ostara
19-22 March

Lughnasadh
1 August

Beltane
1 May

Litha
19-23 June

https://commons.wikimedia.org/wiki/File:Wheel_of_the_Year.svg

The remaining four festivals indicate the solar calendar – the Spring and Autumn Equinoxes and the Winter and Summer Solstices. Not all Pagan traditions celebrate all eight of these festivals – some celebrate only the Solstices while others celebrate only the Equinoxes – there is no hard and fast rule unless you belong to a Grove that follows all eight.

Let's have a closer look at these festivals.

Samhain – October 31st/November 1st

Also known as Winter Night, Samhain (pronounced as sow'inn) is the Pagan calendar's most important date. Why? It's because it marks the passing of a year and the birthing of a new one for many Pagans. Some will choose Imbolc as their new year.

Samhain has long been celebrated in Britain for many centuries, and the Irish Iron Age Celts celebrated it as their most important festival, a time when the Otherworld Gods mingled and walked with men. The celebrations included feasts where men would boast of their battle conquests, displaying their conquests' tongues mounted on sticks as proof.

When the Romans invaded Britain, additional elements were added to the celebration – Roman harvest celebrations where the fruit tree Goddess, Pomona, was honored. Later, the Christians attempted to replace the Pagan Festivals. Samhain became known as All Saints Day, better known as All Hallows Eve or Hallowe'en, where Christian Gods were recognized instead of the Pagan gods.

For most people, what we know as Hallowe'en today is likely all that remains of the ancient festival, but Pagans still retain some historical elements in their celebrations. Death is still the key theme, but it is not morbid by any stretch of the imagination. Pagans do not fear death; they value old age for its wisdom, and they accept death as part of the cycle of life, death, and birth. When they celebrate Samhain, they remember loved ones who have passed and sometimes even invite their spirits to join the celebrations.

Death is also a symbol of endings, so Pagans often reflect on the passing of a job, a relationship, and other parts of life that have ended to make way for a new one. What has passed is sanctified, and life can go on. Samhain is seen as heralding in disorder and darkness, and modern pagans treat it as a time when the boundaries separating the living from the dead are at their thinnest.

Practicing pagans develop personal rituals to contact the dead and the divine. Feasting tends to be a large part of the celebrations, and pagans will even dwell on the time when the Celtic festivals were full of debauchery, indulging in large amounts of food and alcohol. Others are frugal in their food and alcohol intake, some avoiding alcohol altogether. Many are vegetarian or vegan, and others support free-range and organic farming methods as their way of expressing their gratitude and veneration of nature.

Beltane – April 30th/May 1st

Also known as May Eve, the Celtic word, Beltane translates as "Fires of Bel." Bel was one of the Celtic deities, and Beltane is a fire festival, celebrating summer arriving and a fertile year ahead. Celtic festivals often revolve around what the community needs and the spring heralds the start of the farming calendar. Farmers and the rest of the community hope for a fruitful harvest for everyone.

Fire festivals were used to cleanse and purify and hopefully increase the chances of fertility. Often, cattle were passed between fires, with flame and smoke properties thought to ensure the herd was fertile. Today, fire is still a critical part of many Beltane festivals, with lots of different traditions. Fire is thought to be a purifier, cleansing and revitalizing, and at many celebrations, people will jump over the Beltane fire. Many believe this will bring them good fortune, a fertile mind, spirit, body, and happiness for the year ahead.

The biggest of the United Kingdom Beltane celebrations is held in Edinburgh, where fires are lit in the evening, and the celebrations continue through the night until dawn breaks. However, private celebrations happen all over the United Kingdom, with fires being lit and covens and groves celebrating the beginning of summer.

Often, Beltane rituals included courting. Young women and men would collect blossoms from the woods and light fires at nightfall. Often, rituals such as these would lead to good matches followed by marriages in the summer or fall. Today, modern pagans believe that the God Bel becomes strong and mature enough to court the Goddess and become her lover at Beltane.

Overall, what happens with the farming and the fields have primarily become insignificant to modern pagans, but fertility is still a big issue. Sexual imagery plays a big part, and maypole dancing at Beltane is still very popular. Others look at fertility in a different light, in terms of having a creative and active life. After all, if we are to succeed in work, family, and personal interests, we must have fertile minds.

Lughnasadh – August 2nd/4th

Often known as Freysfest or Lammas, Lughnasadh (pronounced as loo-nass-ah) falls at the start of August, about the same time as the Celts celebrated the Irish God Lugh. Some pagan traditions call it Lammas or Freysfest, in remembrance of hleafmass (loaf mass,) an Anglo-Saxon festival also held at the same time.

Agricultural communities saw this as the first harvest day, a time when the fields would be alight with corn, and they would begin reaping. This period carried on until Samhain, the last day of the harvest, a time when the final stores would be put away for winter.

Farming is not such an essential part of modern life (although it should be), but Lughnasadh is still celebrated as a harvest festival, and the rites still contain symbols of corn reaping.

Imbolc – February 1st/2nd

Also known as Disfest, Oimelc, or Candlemas, Imbolc (pronounced as imolk) was an important festival for the Celts and was associated with the new dawning of life and light. The Celts held the farming season in high importance, and success was paramount to them. By now, stores of winter foods would be getting low, so rituals were carried out to bring in divine energy, thus ensuring that what food they had would last until the new harvest six months later.

As with many of the Celtic festivals, Imbolc revolves around fires being lit to celebrate the sun's ever-increasing strength for the next few months. Initially, those fires were used to burn the decorations from Yule, along with any other unwanted items – this is where we get our "ritual" of spring-cleaning. Now, people take their Christmas decorations down by 12th night (January 6th), but in the early ages, the celebrations would run from Yule right up to Candlemas. The Yule log was used to light candles and torches, which would then be carried around the community in a procession.

This was also Brigid's holy day, the Goddess of Fire, fertility, and healing, but the Christians changed this to St. Bridget's Day. Candlemas became a time when worshippers celebrated the Purification of the Virgin Mary by offering lit candles blessed and sprinkled with holy water over them in her honor.

Pagans still see Imbolc as a significant time. Because of their deep connection with nature and the natural world, they recognize that both heat and cold, life and death, share strength. When reflecting on nature, many pagans believe in human action. As the world wakes up from its winter slumber, it is time to do the things we have no time for in the busier times of the year - planting flowers, making candles, telling stories, and reading poetry.

Spring/Vernal Equinox March 20th/21st

The spring equinox is a celebration of the renewed life spring brings to the world. A solar festival, it is celebrated when the day and night are of equal length. This happens twice a year (spring and autumn equinoxes,) and the Celts celebrated the turning seasons with different festivities. Some pagans call it the Ostara festival, after Ostra or Eostre, a Teutonic Goddess, and that name also gave rise to Easter, a Christian festival that celebrates Jesus's life.

Today, the start of spring is still celebrated by pagans. All the changes taking place in the world are attributed to their God and Goddess's powers increasing. At this time, the God is often called The Green Man, and the Goddess is often called Mother Earth. Some say that The Green Man was born of Mother Earth during the winter and may live until Samhain when he dies.

Pagans carry out certain rituals at the spring equinox. For example, a man and woman are chosen to play the Spring God and Goddess roles. They play out a courtship and plant seeds as a form of symbolism. Other traditional activities include hunting eggs, egg races, painting eggs, and eating them, and remember these things were done long before the Christians claimed this time of year as Easter.

Summer Solstice – June 21st (Occasionally June 24th)

Sometimes called Midsummer or Litha, the summer solstice celebrates the longest day, the time when the Sun is at its highest point. Solstice translates to "standing still or stopping of the Sun," and the Celts would light bonfires to add energy to the Sun while the Christians celebrated the Feast of St John the Baptist. It is also a Chinese festival celebrating Li, the Goddess of Light (in China).

Pagans revere the Sun's strength, as do many other religious groups, along with the divine powers responsible for creating life. This is a significant spoke in the Wheel of the Year for pagans. At the start of spring, the Goddess took the reins of the Earth, and now, at the summer solstice, her powers and fertility are at their height. This marks the marriage between the God and Goddess, a union seen as the driving force behind the fruits of the harvest. The solstice is a time for celebrating life and growth, and pagans, deeply aware of the world's balance and the seasonal shifts, tend to settle on diverse traditions to celebrate it. Thousands of people in England, both pagan and non-pagan, visit ancient sites of religion, like Avebury and Stonehenge, to watch the sun rise on the first day of summer.

Autumn Equinox – September 20th/21st

Sometimes called Harvest Home, Mabon, or Fallfest, this equinox is also when the days and nights are the same lengths. Only, this time, instead of heralding the longer days, we herald the end of the harvest season, the time when the days get shorter and descend into darkness. Nature's activity begins to slow down, preparing for winter's hibernation, and it also heralded the time of the fruit harvest. Many pagans use this solstice as a time to reflect on the season that has gone by, and it is also used to recognize that the balance has changed; the wheel continues to turn, and summer is gone. If you are a keen astrologer, you will know that the autumn equinox happens on the day when the Sun enters Libra, and we all know that Libra's sign is the balanced scales. While harvest festivals are often held to give thanks to the Goddess for sufficient food for the winter, this is not one of the most celebrated festivals.

Winter Solstice – December 20th/21st

Otherwise known as Midwinter or Yule, the Winter Solstice celebrates the returning of the light. This is the shortest day of the year when the night is longest. But, from this point on, the Sun's strength begins to grow, and the days lengthen. In ancient times, the dark turning to light was worthy of rejoicing because it assured us we would once again see the spring, the heat, and the growth.

This was when the Great Mother, the Queen of Heaven, birthed the Son of Light. Yet another festival involving lighting fires, people sought to increase the sun's power and mark that summer was triumphing over winter, that light was slowly beating darkness back.

Eisteddfod

Eisteddfod is one of the largest and one of the oldest Welsh culture celebrations, and every year the Eisteddfod comes to a different part of Wales. The word literally translates to "a sitting," possibly referencing the hand-carved chair that the best poet wins in the "Crowning of the Bard" ceremony.

The National Eisteddfod of Wales can be traced back to 1176, when thought the first-ever ceremony was held. Lord Rhys invited musicians and poets from across Wales to attend a gathering at his Cardigan castle. The best musician and poet were awarded a chair at the Lord's Table, and that tradition continues to this day.

After 1176, Eisteddfodau were held all over Wales, with Welsh noblemen and gentry as the patrons. It soon developed into one of the largest folk festivals ever, although popularity declined in the 18th century. Early in the 19th century, a revival began, and 1880 saw the National Eisteddfod Association's formation. Since then, with the exceptions of 1914 and 1940, the Eisteddfod has happened every year.

In 1819, Gorsedd y Beirdd (the Gorsedd of Bards) first appeared when the Eisteddfod was held in Carmarthen at the Ivy Bush Inn. To this day, it remains closely associated with the festival. The Gorsedd is an association made up of writers, poets, artists, musicians, and any individual whose contribution to the Welsh culture, language, and literature was significant. The association members are all Druids, and their ranks are denoted by their costume colors – blue, white, and green.

The Archdruid heads the Gorsedd and is elected for three years at a time. He conducts the ceremonies throughout Eisteddfod week. Each ceremony honors certain literary achievements amongst Welsh prose writers and poets, and there are three Gorsedd ceremonies:

- **The Crowning (Coroni)** – the best poet, as judged in free meter in the competition, is crowned

- **The Awarding of the Prose Medal** – to whoever wins the Prose competitions

- **The Chairing (Cadeiro)** – to the bard who produces the best long poem

The Archdruid stays on the Eisteddfod stage during the ceremonies, with the Gorsedd of Bards, all wearing their ceremonial robes. When the Archdruid is ready to speak the winning poet's name, a trumpet (Corn Gwlad) calls everyone together. Everyone chants the Gorsedd Prayer while the Archdruid draws a sword three times, shouting, "Is there peace?" The assembly will reply, "peace" to this call.

A young, married, local woman then presents the Archdruid with the Horn of Plenty and urges him to drink the "wine of welcome" while another girl presents a basket containing "flowers from the land and soil of Wales." A floral dance then takes place, based on a flower-gathering pattern. These ceremonies are unique to the National Eisteddfod and Wales.

This isn't all Eisteddfod is about, though. Another side of it is maes yr Eisteddfod, which translates to "the Eisteddfod field." Here, there are draft, book, music, food stalls and radio shows, and music competitions in the Theatr y Maes, translated to the "theater on the field." Here, you will also find tents for Literature, Society, and a live music tent, which is always popular, but only Welsh songs in the Welsh language can be performed. There is also a learner's tent for Welsh Language students and teachers.

Every year, Welsh people return to Wales from wherever they are in the world to participate in a welcoming ceremony during the Eisteddfod. Wales International organizes the ceremony held on the Thursday of the Eisteddfod at the Eisteddfod Pavilion.

In Patagonia, South America, Eisteddfod is held twice a year in Trelew and Gaiman towns in the Chubut Province. This started in the 1880s and consists of poetry, recitation, music competitions, all in the Welsh language, and Spanish and English. A silver crown is presented to the person who wins Best Poem in Spanish, while the Best Poet in Welsh is honored with a full religious ceremony that asks for health and peace. The Chairing of the Bard involves presenting a large ornately carved wooden chair. The Trelew Eisteddfod attracts visitors from across the world and is a large gathering.

Chapter 4: Meditate and Pray the Druid Way

Meditation has long been an approach to Druid tradition, and although it is similar to many other meditation methods, there is one major difference – attitude and mindset. More specifically, this is in your thinking mind's attitude. Most meditation practices will teach students they should stop thinking – they should do this by using mantras or through symbolic visualization or by focusing their attention on the Koans of Zen or other paradoxes that stop their thought.

This is quite an effective way of getting yourself into a meditative state of unconsciousness. Still, there is a downside to it – it can cause many mystics to enter into profound spiritual states but who cannot think clearly.

By contrast, Druid meditation takes another path – the path of retraining the mind and reorienting it rather than closing it down altogether. Like many other mystical traditions, Druidry recognizes that when you divorce reason from reality and when you divorce it from other valid human experience forms, you enter into a form of madness. Since Pythagoras's time, many Western sages and mystics have also come to recognize that the mind and the spirit need not be enemies. We need to learn how to bring the mind into harmony with itself and with the human self that the mind is a part of, not to mention the cosmos. The rational is the spiritual's vehicle, the promise, and premise of many of the Western paths of mysticism. The Druids adopted this approach right at the start of the Druid revival.

Central to all of this is thinking meditatively, which takes a lot of practice. Like anything, the more you practice, the better you will be and the more effective. If you really want to get good at it, you need to practice every day.

This kind of meditation is called discursive meditation – we don't stop the thinking process; we simply clarify it and redirect it. We don't abolish our thoughts; we make them into a vehicle for consciousness. Typically, we do this by focusing our minds on something specific, and we allow our minds to play out that topic, play out the implications through ideas while maintaining focus on the topic. When we do this, we gradually transform our thinking from constant, random chatter into a focused and powerful method of understanding. The knowledge we gain from this has its own set of good values.

The meditator must focus on an idea or an image of their choosing – this is the meditation theme. The meditator follows the theme giving it careful consideration, following the implications of it and the consequences. They must restrain their mind when it tries to think about something else and allow it to follow their chosen theme freely as far as possible. This has two effects, both positive. First, it teaches you how to master awareness and attention. Where most other forms of meditation fail, it also teaches you how to understand mediation themes far deeper than normal thinking ever does.

It's more than just that, though. A good deal of the Druid teachings, symbols, and myths were, and still are, designed to reveal their meanings only to those who have taught themselves focused and careful attention. Discursive meditation is a key part of the Druid's inner dimensions.

There are valuable preliminaries, and the most important is choosing the meditation theme. Every part of a Druid's study, every part of their practice can give them a theme, and the most common sources come from books they have studied. Beginners often make the monumental mistake of picking too broad a theme, and they do one of two things – skim over it or flounder. Either way, they are missing the point and the depth of the practice. Generally, if your theme cannot be described in a short sentence, you cannot use it for a single meditation – split it down into several smaller themes, and then you can recombine them all later.

How to Meditate

What you meditate on is not the only important thing – how you meditate is also crucial. Start by sitting on a chair. It should not have a cushioned seat, just a plain chair, and be seated far enough forward that your lower back does not rest against the chair back. Place your feet flat on the floor and straighten up without stiffening your back. Your head should be held upright and not slumped, and your hands rested on your thighs, palms down, with your elbows tucked against your thighs.

Unlike the Eastern mediation systems, where meditators are seated cross-legged on the floor, this system allows your energies to remain unsealed, open to the cosmos, which is one of the most critical parts of the spiritual Druidry practice. That is because Druids are never alone and always part of the larger world and universe.

Most people choose the same time and place to meditate daily. If you have a variable schedule, it is useful to choose the same point in your schedule before breakfast. Try to face east when meditating since it allows you to benefit from the currents in the Earth's subtle body. And to complete your meditation setting, you should have a clock you can see without moving your head.

When you are comfortably in position, relax your body, one part at a time, consciously. Start at your feet and move up your body one part at a time. Then spend time focusing consciously on your breath, ensuring you breathe slowly and evenly in and out. One of the best exercises to do here is called the Fourfold Breath. Breathe in slowly, counting in your head up to four. Breathe out to a mental count of four, and then, when your lungs are empty, hold your breath out, counting up to four again. Repeat the exercise, counting at the same pace throughout, and hold your breath (in and out) using your diaphragm and chest muscles – do NOT close your throat because this can lead to health issues.

Focus on your breathing for about five minutes, and then focus on your meditation theme. Silently state the theme to yourself in as few words as possible or use a single image to visualize it. Focus on it for a few minutes and then begin to think about it. Turn the theme over in your mind, and think about its implications and the connections. Then, choose the one that most appeals to you. Follow it as far as possible, but when (if) your thoughts begin to stray, and they will, don't bring them straight back to your theme. Instead, follow those thoughts back to where you were in your theme and stay there, continuing. In time, you will find this much easier to do.

One important thing you should do is set a time limit for your meditation in advance. Stick to that limit even if you feel you've gone nowhere. A good length, to begin with, is five minutes of breathing exercises and 10 of meditation. When your session is finished, do the Fourfold Breath or focus on your breath again for a minute or two –

this will make sure you can easily get back to your normal state of awareness.

The Ancestor Altar

We set the ancestor altar up, not to worship our ancestors but to remember them and honor them. You can also use this altar for any purpose, including ceremonies, rituals, meditations, and more.

Choose where you will set up the altar - it can be a dresser, mantle, table, and so on. Now choose four crystals or stones. One goes on each corner of the altar to represent the world's four corners. You will also need a water carafe or decanter to hold the spirit water - this is a combination of spring water and white rum, blessed by you. Include family pictures or objects that belonged to or will represent the family member. It's up to you if you use an altar cloth or not, but if you do, it should be fringed as this is traditional. Fringes are a way of connecting your consciousness and your ancestor's consciousness. Your altar table should also contain an abalone shell because this represents Mother Earth's womb.

There are three ancestor classes - blood, spiritual linage, and land. You can choose to honor any or all of them. One way of honoring land ancestors is to have a pot full of Earth on your altar while honoring the spiritual ancestors. This could be done by having an object on your altar with your spiritual path's symbol on it, i.e., Awen for the Druids.

Ancestor Altar Dedication

Prepare drinks and food that would have appealed to your chosen ancestor in life, and use them as an offering. You must state an intention so the space you are honoring them in is sacred. Ask for their help - there is no need to include every ancestor, but state that the only ancestors welcome are those that come in peace and love and wish no harm.

When you dedicate the altar, at the initial feast and for any future offerings (remember your ancestors with drink and food regularly), bless the food and say:

O blood of my blood, this is your child (name yourself). I bring you (name the food/drink) for your nourishment. Know that you are loved and respected. Accept this offering for our good. Watch over your descendant: Let there be no death, let there be no illness, let there be no accident, let there be no upheaval, let there be no poverty, let there be no ill-fate (name any other attributes you wish to dispel). Stand fast for me, for my good fortune, for my wealth, for my happiness, for my home, for my health (name any other attributes you wish to attract). Thank you, blood of my blood. Thank you, O mighty dead.

Other Prayers: (from Luisah Teisch)

O good and mighty dead, you who wish me only good, hear me; guide and guard me, and when the time comes, greet me. You are neither blind nor deaf to this life I live; you did yourself once share it. I come to you in love and trust. I seek to honor you.

A Prayer for the Living:

To my kindred (name all you wish to remember)

May the blessing of the spirit be upon you.

May you be your best self.

May you walk in beauty.

May your guides be with you at every crossroads,

May you be honorably greeted when you arrive.

Three Kindreds Prayer Beads

These Prayer Beads devotional is far more Druid in content than many other versions, and it honors the Three Kindreds – Ancestors (the Ancient Dead spirits), Earth Spirits (those who share the world), and the Gods (the Shining Ones.)

String your beads yourself, if you can, rather than purchasing them.

You will need:

- 13 * 8mm white beads – these are for the Gods and the Goddesses
- 13* 8mm red beads – these are for the Earth spirits
- 13 * 8mm black beads – these are for the Ancestors
- 1 * 10mm silver bead – to represent the Sun
- 52 * spacer beads (silver, class E 6/0) to represent the Sunlight
- Clear mono-filament nylon thread

It doesn't matter where you start and finish, but if you end in the middle of the black beads, the tie-off doesn't show so much.

The silver bead should be kept separate from the white beads using four spacer beads. A spacer follows each white bead, but bead 13 must have four spacers after it. The red beads follow this, each with one spacer after it, and again, place four spacers after the 13th bead. Repeat with the black beads.

It should be that each bead of the same color has one spacer between, and each set of colors has four spacers between. We use 13 beads to signify the 13 months of the lunar cycle, and the spacers are silver to represent the Druid Sun issuing light through the Three Kindreds.

Say the prayers below on each bead, at the same time practicing mediation on the mysteries of the kindreds and human life experiences:

Prayers For Your Druid Beads

On the gold Sun Bead say:

Blessed (Father, Mother,) come to me,

and cast your lovely, golden light.

Give light to Earth that I may see

your glory shining ever bright.

Triple Kindred, Blessed Be,

and true well met, my soul's delight!

On the space say:

I bind unto myself today the

Memory of the Ancestors.

Meditate on the Memory of the Ancestors . . .

On each Ancestor Bead say:

Ancestors, Ancient Ones,

Remember me as I remember you

Old Ones, hear my prayer,

And accept my offering of love.

On the space say:

I bind unto myself today the

Comradeship of all Earth Spirits

Meditate on the Aid of the Earth Spirits . . .

On each Earth Spirit Bead say:

Fur and feather, leaf and stone,

Aid me as I aid you.

Earth Spirits hear my prayer,

And accept my offering of love.

On the space say:

I bind unto myself today the
Power of the Gods and Goddesses.

Meditate on the Honor of the Shining Ones . . .

On each God and Goddess Bead say:

Gods and Goddesses, Shining Ones,
Honor me as I honor you.
First-Born of Earth, hear my prayer,
And accept my offering of love.

On the space say:

I bind unto myself today
The Presence of the Three Kindreds.

On the gold Sun Bead conclude:

I bind unto myself today
The virtues of the starlit Heavens,
The glorious Sun's life-giving ray,
The whiteness of the Moon at even;
The flashing of the lightning free,
The whirling Wind's tempestuous shocks;
The stable Earth, the deep salt Sea,
Around the old eternal Rocks.
So may it be.

Other Prayers

Invoking the Holy Ancestors

Hail Lady of the Lake and the Merlyn of Britain,

Ancestors of those who follow the path of the

Order of the Northern Way. I summon and stir thee!

Come and be welcome in this holy place.

Here, make the sign of the hammer and/or the Three Rays

To the Ancestors who have gone before me,

come and be welcomed as my honored guests in this holy place.

Repeat the sign.

Greeting the New Moon

May thy light be fair to me!

May thy course be smooth to me!

If good to me is thy beginning,

Seven times better be thine end,

Thou fair moon of the seasons,

Thou great lamp of grace!

He Who created thee

Created me likewise;

He Who gave thee weight and light

Gave to me life and death,

And the joy of the seven satisfactions,

Thou great lamp of grace,

Thou fair moon of the seasons.

The Druid Vow

We swear by peace and love to stand,

Heart to heart and hand in hand.

Mark, O Spirit, and hear us now,
Confirming this, our sacred vow.

Chapter 5: Rites and Rituals

One of the most important parts of Druid tradition are the rites of passage – it is these that allow us to mark change, acknowledge growth, and give ourselves release. Some rites have their own variants in many spiritual and religious traditions, such as funerals, weddings, naming ceremonies, and more. But other rites are specific to certain paths, like initiation ceremonies.

It is important to understand that rites and rituals are not only a part of nature-based spirituality or Druidry; they are a part of our whole lives. A leading scholar called Catherine Bell published a book named "Ritual: Perspectives and Dimensions," where she states that, for as long as history has been recorded, humans have participated in rituals. And they were likely doing so even before any historical records!

Rituals involve the use of movement, symbols, repetitive forms, actions, and staging to prepare us to step out of normal time with sacred intention consciously. Not all rituals are about religion or spiritualism; many are personal or about culture, such as graduation ceremonies.

Rituals are a great way of helping us connect with the Earth and ourselves. They help us raise energy, mark events, and so much more. Every culture has rituals, although each will look and manifest itself differently. Druid tradition, specifically revival Druidry, often involves rituals for lots of different things, including but not limited to:

- Marking and celebrating seasonal holidays, such as the equinoxes, solstices, new moons, cross-quarter days, full moons, and so on

- Raising the energy to heal the land, bless it, and honor it

- Raising the energy for your personal work

- Opening sacred spaces for sacred communion with the land, bardic creation, meditation, and so on

- Seeking guidance or assistance

- Lowering the energy for different reasons, including land healing, shadow work, removing sickness, and palliative care work, to name a few

- Practices of gratitude

A Ritual Creation Framework

Now I will tell you, step-by-step, how to create your own rituals:

Step One: Intention

Before you start, you need to determine what your goal for this ritual is or your purpose. Ask yourself two questions – what is your intention, and what do you want to accomplish? Knowing this is the biggest determiner in what you do and how it's done. There are many goals for seeking a ritual. You might have a couple in mind for yours, for example, blessing a park or celebrating a holiday in the best way for you.

Step Two: Framework

Every tradition has a form of structure or framework used to understand the power sources, interpret the world, or categorize it. These frameworks are often aligned closely to or are the same as the energy sources (you will understand this when you get to step four.)

Recognize that if you are already using a sacred space, circle, or grove to open and close your rituals, you already have the framework and can move on to step three. Know you need not use full opening and closing rituals for every ritual, but to use them, remember that you need to know if you want to create your own or use existing openings and closings.

Broad Druid Frameworks

• The Four Elements – Earth, Fire, Water, and Air (or it could be five if you use Spirit.) These elements have been a big part of Western tradition for over 2500 years, most likely for a lot longer.

• The Celtic tradition framework of Earth, sea, and sky

• The Druid revival Gwyar/Calas/Nyfre framework

• The Druid animals connected to directions – North (the great bear), South (the stag), East (the hawk), and West (the salmon)

AODA-Specific Frameworks

• The seven-element framework is the primary one, consisting of Air, Water, Earth, Fire (the four classic elements,) and the Spirit Within/Above/Below (the three spirit aspects)

• You could replace the three spirit aspects with the currents – Lunar, Telluric, and Solar.

You will also need:

- **Something Related to Your Tradition** – Some people combine two or more traditions to their spiritual path. If this is you, use any framework from any of your traditions, including deities, and so on.

- **Something Unique or Local to You** – In time, you will probably develop a framework of your own. These may be developed into something that resonates with your practice, or you may choose a framework that does the same, for example, sacred animals, four sacred mountains, and so on.

Step Three: Consideration of Marking, Opening and Closing your Sacred Space, and of a Formal or Informal Ritual

There is one thing you need to consider – whether your grove opening and closing will be a formal part of your ritual. That leads to a question – when should you use formal or informal openings?

You need to understand why you even use grove openings and closings, and I'll tell you now. There are three reasons at the very least. The first reason is psychological – we need a way to help mark the differences between sacred or spiritual time and your daily life. If you are a part of a dominant religion, for example, the best way of achieving this to go to a different physical location, wear specific clothes, and if it is a Christian religion, begin with a prayer or a song. In the neo-pagan and Druid traditions, there are few physical buildings to choose from, so a grove or circle opening is the best way of designating the difference between sacred and mundane space and time.

The second is all about your connection to and relationship with the spirit world and your tradition. Repeating specific traditions will transform them into deep, meaningful rituals. For instance, if you repeat the same grove opening and closing for many years, it will have more emotional and symbolic meaning. The more you do these ritual forms, the more effective they become. As you engage with these rituals, you build up meaning, making the energy and the imagery a part of you.

The third is about the roots of many traditions - the occult. When doing magical or energetic work, we create a sacred space - our work must be protected from external influence. The spirit world is not all about love and light. Many things can be attracted to the energy, and not all of those things are good. When you set boundaries between you and the rest of the world, you can protect against those bad external influences.

So, with those three reasons, the question now is - when do you use formal openings? First up, it's all about your intention and what you are doing. A formal ritual tends to be used when you celebrate the big holidays and any work where you want to raise energy and direct it, do magical work, blessings, etc. an informal ritual is the smaller things you do when you need to like your daily practices, such as celebrating something, offering gratitude, and so on; these do not need formal rituals.

For example, let's say that you want to open your meals with a ritual - an informal one will do just fine. But to bless your garden for the entire growing season, it would be better to do a formal ritual.

One of the most important factors is context. If you are out in public or with people who do not have the same beliefs as you, it may not be possible to use a formal opening to do your ritual work. If you wanted to do a tree blessing in a busy park, you couldn't go through a full formal opening, but if you chose to do the same thing in your garden, you could. With the park scenario, you could do a blessing ritual, opening the sacred space in advance. You would then embed your blessing in a stone or something similar. Take the stone to the park with you, leave it at the tree, and play a bit of music or say a few quiet words. What I'm saying is, the context will determine if a formal ritual makes sense or not.

One last thing to consider is when to use ritual clothing and tools. Formal rituals usually involve dressing in ritual clothes, using an altar, and throwing yourself into it. Informal rituals rarely require many, if any, tools or special clothing. You can carry grove stones with you, wherever you go, if you want to perform a ritual.

Step Four: Energy, Assistance, and Guidance Sources

Often, a ritual is more effective when you have an energy, guidance, or assistance source external to you that can be called upon. As mentioned in step two, this can be with or separate from the framework.

Energy Sources

You need not use energy sources for every ritual, but you do need them where you are attempting to affect the world with a blessing or healing ritual. Were you greeting the Sun with a simple honoring ceremony, you wouldn't need one because you have one – the Sun. But if you wanted to bless a journey, you would need to send external energy in your ritual.

Why is this so important? Every one of us has internal energy that can be called upon. The problem is that energy is not infinite; the more we take, the quicker we deplete the energy. If you have external energy sources you can draw on, then the rituals will have more meaning and far more impact because you can lend them power, strength, and extra energy.

Sources you can draw on include:

- The energy within you

- Energy from activity, music, or movement generated by you

- Energy from your frameworks, such as Ogham trees, four elements, three druid elements, and seven elements

- Energy from sacred timings, such as equinoxes, solstices, and moons

- Energy from around you, in the natural world, like the mountains, herbs, plants, trees, and stones

- Energy from connections to a deity or spirits

- Energy from sacred spaces you have built and cultivate

Assistance or Guidance Sources

Some rituals look for external guidance or assistance, perhaps because you need advice on your life's challenges or a specific direction to take. You may even want to ask a deity or spirit to help you with your work. These sources come in several forms, including:

- Systems of divination, such as Ogham, Runes, Tarot, and Pendulums

- Guides, spirits, and deities

- From nature, either something specific or broader

- Your higher self or subconscious

Should you decide to use these in any ritual, think carefully about how you will call it in and honor it. For the deities, nature, or the guides, this should be done respectfully, with offerings and gratitude. Even if you use a divination system, honor the tool, not just use it.

Step Five: Methods to Use

Now we can talk about the methods of achieving your intentions or goals. This is by no means an exhaustive list, but it does show you where to start:

Setup Your Ritual Space

Your ritual space is important in helping with your ritual preparations, and things to consider are:

- Will your ritual be held in or outdoors?

- Will it be held in an already established space, a sacred space you often use in your rituals, or are you creating a new one?

- What will help you set up for the ritual? Think about decorations you want to use, seasonal materials, incense, candles, an altar, and so on.

- Are you going to wear ritual or special clothing?

- Will your ritual include a feast? Will you be making offerings? What will it include?

- If others are included in your ritual, make sure that everyone has a way of sharing or adding to the sacred space. For example, if you are doing a Samhain ritual, everyone could add an ancestral photo or object to the altar.

Make sure you take the time to set your ritual space up for formal rituals. Your space is a critical part of developing a meaningful ritual with a real impact. Think of it as like having a dinner party. The space has to be right - the table must look good, the house clean, and the food must be exceptional. If you hosted a party with poor food, a poorly laid table, and a dirty house, it just wouldn't be right.

Methods to Raise Energy

These methods are used for blessing, healing, creating bardic arts, and empowering. These methods include:

- **Chanting** - Using Awen or Ogham words is a great choice. Chanting magic is an incredibly powerful way of accomplishing rituals and goals.

- **Body and Dance Movement** - This method is used in lively rituals, where participants drum, dance, and move about to raise the energy for something specific. You don't have to be part of a group for this - it works just as well when you are alone.

- **Making Noise, Drumming, and Clapping** - This raises energy far quicker than most other methods, so don't be afraid to make as much noise as you need to.

• **Using Words** – Inviting or calling forth, no matter what, words are powerful. It can be highly effective to state your intention and what your work is.

• **Herbs, Oils, and Plants** – These can be very powerful methods to raise energy, even more so if you connect with the plant, herb, or oil.

Lowering or Removing Methods

In the same way you need to do work to raise the energy, you also need to do it when you want to lower or remove it. Removal is typically used when doing land healing, self-development, or trying to drop bad habits. These methods include:

• **Drumming Down** - start drumming fast and slow the beat down until it comes to a stop

• **Ritual Burning** – herbs, papers, words, etc.

• **Casting Off** – by casting an energy-imbued object off (into a lake or river, for example) or by burying it

• **Cleansing/Clearing** – using herbs, vinegar, or salt – fumitory herbs can be used in smoke cleansing or vinegar/salt in water cleansing

Gratitude Practices

Showing gratitude and honoring is another important part of ritual work. An offering was traditionally something that would cost the giver like fruits of a harvest, labor, and winter food. Offerings are not just meant to be symbolic. They should be useful and meaningful too, and these are a few ways you can do this:

• **Physical Offerings** – Include wine, cake, incense, herbal blends, etc. You might think these are the easy way out, but you need to consider something. When you make your offering, it should be mindful of nature and not destroy the planet.

- **Service Offerings** – Include planting a tree, changing your lifestyle, cleaning up the trash, etc. Given the challenges we have faced in recent times, these are possibly some of the best offering forms. If you make your offering in a ritual setting, state what it is – whether you have done it or plan to.

- **Bardic Offerings** – Includes chanting, dancing, music, etc. These are welcome offerings, partly because they take no physical resources and partly because you can use sacred intent with them.

- **Bodily Offerings** – Can include liquid gold, hair, etc. When you do a ritual spontaneously, you may have nothing to offer. Hair is one of the more traditional offerings, and while you might be wondering where you can get hold of liquid gold, you already have it – urine. This offering can go to the base of a tree (never on a plant directly) because it is nitrogen. You can even offer your breath, as it is rich in carbon.

Step Six: Solitary or Group

Before we put our ritual together, there is one more thing to do – decide whether you are going it alone or with a group. If you are doing it by yourself, you can skip ahead to step seven. If you are joining with others, keep reading, as these are things you need to consider:

- If you are working with people you know, such as part of a grove, include them in the ritual design, even if it's nothing more than bringing something to it, like spring water.

- Ensure all participants are comfortable – Many people like to be physically involved while others prefer to observe. Ensure that every person does something they want to do, and if they don't have a formal role to play, get them to join in with interacting, visualizing, and other bits of the ritual.

- The ritual should be interactive, and everyone should do something, however small, so long as it is meaningful. Some people say rituals are boring, but those are only the ones where you stand around and listen or watch others doing something. Make yours something different by engaging all participants.

• Provide participants with a memento to make your ritual more powerful. This could be anything tied to the ritual, such as ribbons, seeds, sacred water, and more.

• Make your ritual meaningful, and make sure it has an impact. Think about ways to make the ritual mean something to everyone involved.

• Make sure that everyone is aware of what is happening. Talk through it ahead of time if you can. Show everyone what will go on, the goals, and anything else you think will be helpful.

Step Seven: Structure

Now we reach the final step, putting it all together. These are just a couple of structures that will help you do this:

Formal

Formal rituals tend to be based around the following structure, although you can vary it as required:

• **Open the Space** – Once your space is set up and you are prepared, open it.

• **Declare Your Intentions** – Use the right language to state what the ritual is for and what your intentions are, thus telling everyone else involved what the goal is. This also tells the powers of nature, deity, or spirit what the goals are too.

• **Do the Core Work** – This is wildly variable, and I will give you a few ideas in a minute.

• **Close the Space** – This helps you step back to your daily life, return the energy you didn't use back to the earth, and give thanks.

The core work will depend on what your intention is, but the formula is much the same:

- Gratitude, prayers, or a few words about your intention
- Raise the energy
- Direct the energy
- Give thanks

Informal

Informal structures do not involve opening or closing ceremonies; they just focus on your work. They could include meditation, prayer, offerings, breathwork, and more, and they may also contain things that help you transition quickly, like the Ogham wisdom chant that offers the three breaths.

Ogham Wisdom Chant

This ritual is simple, and you can use it whenever you need it, even at a moment's notice. The chant's intention is to offer daily strength, wisdom, and discernment when you need it. Its framework and energy source are the Ogham, and its work is to raise the energy needed through chanting.

Here is the ritual:

Breathe in deeply three times and put your hands over your chest

Chant the Oak Ogham three times:

Duir, Duir, Duir (pronounced doo-er)

Breathe in deeply again three times.

This may all seem like quite a lot but given time and practice; you will soon do it all intuitively. These steps are great for beginners, though, considering it walks them through everything one step at a time.

Herbal Grief Ritual to Heal the Soul

2020 was an incredibly challenging year for most people, in more ways than one, and 2021 hasn't exactly started on a good footing either. Many people have faced the worst – losing loved ones, family, and friends – and are struggling with their grief right now. And it's not just grief over what they have lost; it's about the uncertainty of the future, losing a job they loved, a way of life they may never get back, and some are grieving over the damage we, the human race, are doing to our planet.

Grief is a natural process, a part of how we let go. People say that time heals all wounds, but that can only happen if you allow yourself the time to do it. Take the time you need to honor your loss, acknowledge how you feel, and begin the process of healing yourself. If you don't do this and you try to bury your grief deep inside you, it will start to feel like a huge weight that holds you down and holds you back. Now and again, it will come to the surface, but unless you deal with it accordingly, it will just keep coming back. The longer you leave it, the harder it gets.

One of the most powerful ways to deal with grief and help you heal is a ritual. Using sage, rosemary, and thyme in the ritual helps ease your spirit and lets you begin the process of grieving properly. Whether you are grieving for a specific person or just feel the time is right to let go of your grief and move on, this ritual can be of great help.

The three herbs chosen for this ritual are powerful and gentle, and most of us have come into contact with them at some point – you may grow them in your garden, or it could just be in the food you eat.

- **Rosemary** – This herb is linked to remembrance, memory, and the past. Rosemary is one of the most potent of the spirit allies, providing us with a reminder to hold what we love and miss in our hearts for all time and move on and look to the future.

- **Sage** – This herb is spiritually powerful and is used to help us ground ourselves, followed by cleansing and clearing. It doesn't matter what type of sage you use since they all work just the same.

- **Thyme** – This herb helps us put our grief into the right space, make time for it, work through it, and learn to accept it in time.

Preparation

Before you can even think about doing this ritual, you need to get prepared.

Materials:

- An herb sachet containing rosemary, thyme, and sage. You can use fresh or dried herbs from your garden or your local farmer's market and tie them with string.
- Three strips of paper – this is for those who have only the crushed herbs for culinary uses. Write the name of one herb on each strip
- A large bowl
- Scissors

Setting

The ideal place for this is in the bathtub or a basin if you don't have a tub. Put the herbs into the tub or basin. Sponge yourself off while sitting in the shower or in a natural setting. Make sure that you are not going to be disturbed for the entire ritual.

Set this up how you want it. Use incense and candles to set the mood for a bath and have photos of the person you are grieving, or objects related to your grief nearby.

The Grief Ritual

Fill your bath or basin with water and light the candles. Add the herbs to the tub and step in. Chant:

Sage, rosemary, and thyme aid me in my grief

Acknowledge your feelings and honor them. Allow yourself to experience them with no reservations or hesitation fully. When you are ready, you can call to the herbs. Here, you have a choice – use the words I give you below or use your own, so long as they follow the theme. As you speak the words, you must feel them coming from your body, mind, and spirit:

Rosemary

Rosemary, aid me in holding my loved one(s) in my memory. What is remembered will live.

Talk of what or who you are grieving for, and feel the rosemary listening to you. After you have spoken your words out loud, stop, and feel the energy from the rosemary. This energy should provide a kind, gentle memory of what/who you have lost.

Sage

Sage, aid me with cleansing and grounding. With your healing energy, let my heart be brightened and less heavy.

After you have spoken the words out loud, stop and feel the energy from the sage. This energy should provide peace and grounding.

Thyme

Thyme heals all wounds. Sacred thyme lend me the strength to accept my grief process, to feel my way through the grief, and know that time will heal.

Once you have spoken these words out loud, stop, and feel the energy from the thyme. This energy should provide a way forward where time will heal your wounds.

When all three herbs have been called, you must allow yourself peace and quiet, giving the herbs the time they need to work on your heart, body, mind, and spirit. Stay soaking in your bath and relax; feel the healing as it works within you and outside of you.

When you think your work is done or your bath water is cold, fill the large bowl with water from the bath. Cut open the herb sachet, and put all the herbs into the bowl of water. Close your eyes, and swirl the water around in the bowl. Then, when you are ready, draw an herbal sprig (or piece of paper) from the bowl.

Whichever herb you draw, that is the message that will help you process your grief and move forward:

- **Sage** – Your focus should be on self-care, specifically spiritual. Regularly meditate, ground yourself, take yourself out into nature, and do spiritual practices daily. Regularly use a sage incense or sage cleansing stick as part of these practices.

- **Rosemary** – Your focus should be on honoring the memory of what or whom you have lost. Do this, so it feels natural to you, whether it is planting trees in memory, creating a memorial altar, doing something creative, or any other way that feels right. Use rosemary in your cooking, grow it in the garden, or have a small pot of it in the house.

- **Thyme** – Embrace the entire grief process, but be kind to yourself while working through it. Create a special space where you can feel and be, and allow yourself the time you need to heal and accept. There is no rush to this process; you must give yourself the time you need to work through it, and if necessary, contact someone else and talk about your feelings.

When the ritual has ended, close it by thanking the plant spirits for their help, get out of the bath, and extinguish the candles.

Spring Equinox Sun Ritual

Alban Eiler, otherwise known as the Spring Equinox, is when dark and light are balanced. Given the world's turmoil through the global pandemic, now is the time to do a balancing ritual to help balance your own life again.

Preparation

We use three Druid elements in this ritual – Gywar, Calas, and Nyfre. All three come from the Druid revival, and the names come from Ancient Welsh, representing three universal principles.

- **Nwyfre** (pronounced as NOO-iv-ruh) translates to "heaven" or "sky." It references the vital energy or life force we all possess and is the "spark of life" that separates the animate from the inanimate.

- **Gwyar** (pronounced as GOO-yar) translates to "blood." It references the concepts of flexibility, flow, motion, fluidity, and change. This is a water-like element, flowing around an obstacle and not crashing against it.

- **Calas** (CAH-lass) translates to "hard" and has a direct to the Ancient Welsh word, "Caled." It is an element of stability, solidity, and grounding.

The interesting thing is that, if you want real balance, your focus cannot be on Calas, the element of grounding. That's probably what you would automatically think of for balance, but you need all three to be balanced. Calas helps us root ourselves and be stable. Gwyar helps us deal with change, moving smoothly past the obstacles. Nwyfre is life – if we can't embrace life, especially now, we can't focus our energies on bringing life into harmony.

We also need three prayers for this and Awen chanting.

Ideally, you will do this ritual in three parts – sunrise, midday, and sunset.

The Ritual

Choose a sacred space you can be in at sunrise, midday, and sunset. Ideally, this would be somewhere you can open your sacred grove and leave it open for you to return to throughout the day. It can be outside, in your bedroom, or anywhere, so long as nobody else will disturb it. You can also set an altar up here if you want.

Also, make sure you have an offering ready to give to the land and her spirits. This is personal, so what and how you do it is entirely up to you.

Sunrise

Early in the morning – as the light is beginning to show – go to the sacred space you chose, open a sacred grove while following your own traditions. You can use the opening used by your tradition or use the Solitary Grove opening from the AODA.

Make your offering, using your own words, and leave it in the space.

As the Sun rises, says these words:

Sunrise is a time when the Sun rises from the earth. The promise of the day is before us. The balance between light and dark is here. We enter the light half of the year, full of promise, and possibility

Pause for a few seconds, observing the Sun, and then say these words:

As the Sun rises with possibility, I call upon this moment to provide me fluidity, flexibility, and the ability to adapt to a radically changing world. I now intone the ancient word for flow: "Gywar (GOO-yar), Gywar, Gwyar.

Repeat this as many times as you feel right about doing so.

Stand up and face the Sun; feel the heat from its rays on your skin. Observe how the light changes throughout the rising and feel all the possibilities of this moment. Note how the wind flows and how the light wakes the land. Spend a little time meditating and recite the following prayer.

Prayer of Flow

Let me be like the waters,

Let me move like the sea,

Let me flow with the currents,

Let my spirit be free

Let me fly like an eagle

Let me buzz like a bee

Let me swim like an otter

Let my spirit be free

When the world is crushing

And I am unable to see

Let me flow like the river,

Let the awen flow in me!

When finished, exit your sacred space and continue with your day until it is time for the next part of the ritual.

Noon

Go back to your sacred space and give yourself a couple of minutes to re-enter your ritual mindset. Do this with deep breathing exercises, which will help with quieting your mind.

Now say these words:

Noon-day is when the power of the Sun is at its zenith. This is when the Sun's rays offer life and vitality to all. As the Sun is at its height, I call upon this moment to provide me vitality, strength, and energy. I now intone the ancient word for the lifeforce, "Nwyfre (NOO-iv-ruh), Nywfre, Nywfre.

Spend a few minutes standing or sitting in the sunlight. Soak up the rays, observe the trees, plants, and the landscape and how they interact with the Sun. If your sacred space is indoors, try to look out of a window to do this. If you feel it is right, dance, do movement meditation, or another kind of movement that revitalizes you. When you feel your work is done, say the Druid's Prayer:

Grant, O Spirits, your protection

And in protection, strength

And in strength, understanding

And in understanding, knowledge

And in knowledge, the knowledge of justice

And in the knowledge of justice, the love of it

And in the love of it, the love of all existences

And in the love of all existences, the love of earth our mother and all Goodness.

Now you can chant three "Awens" (AHH-OH-EN), and feel the revitalization settling inside you.

Leave your space until it is time to return for the final time.

Sunset

Return to your space as the Sun begins to set and is just touching the horizon.

Say these words:

Sunset is a time when the Sun meets the earth. As the Sun enters the Earth's embrace, I call upon this moment to provide me grounding, stability, and peace. I now intone the ancient word for grounding: Calas (CAY-lass), Calas, Calas.

Repeat as much as you feel is right.

Now sit on the ground or lie on it. Feel how solid the ground is and feel the darkness on the landscape as it deepens. Meditate as the darkness falls around you, feel the Earth supporting and grounding you, giving you peace.

When your meditation is over, say the following Peace Prayer:

Deep within the still center of my being may I find peace.

Pause and feel peace inside you

Quietly, within the circle of this grove, may I share peace.

Pause and feel the peace in your sacred space

Gently within the circle of all life, may I radiate peace.

Pause and feel the peace radiating out from you

Finally, close your space as you would in your tradition.

Chapter 6: The Power of Herbs

Disclaimer

I am not a medical professional, and I do not provide you with any medical advice or diagnoses. This chapter is for information only, and if you have any medical issues, see a medical doctor. Even if you choose to use herbal healing, you should seek advice from your doctor before beginning.

Herbal remedies have long been used throughout the world, particularly in ancient times. Sadly, none of the real ancient Celtic books on herbalism have survived, but some medieval manuscripts provide remedies close to what the Iron Age people used.

If we delve into Irish Myth, we find the tale of Airmid, a Goddess who was the daughter of Diancecht, the surgeon deity. She also had a brother, Miach, who, following his father, mastered how to reattach severed limbs and do organ transplants. Miach was killed after an argument in the family, and on his grave, at least 365 herbs grew. Airmid gathered these and put them on a cloak, each herb laid over the body part it worked on. Her father was terrified that her knowledge would find its way to mortal hands, and he scattered all the herbs. Airmid was the only one who knew what each herb did, and popular speculation says that the early healers used all the herbs, learning how each worked and how to use it. The number of herbs suggests a link to the calendar – one herb for each day. For many thousands of years, astrology continued affecting medicine, and it's possible that the Druids used it to diagnose or treat illnesses.

Brigid is another Goddess with an association with healing. Brigid has three sisters, and one of those is called "The Healer." There is a Gaelic word, lus, which means flame, and that is also the word used for healing herbs. One specific plant named after Brigid is the dandelion.

In early Gaelic society, besides healers with formal training, many people would also have been taught basic healing through information and remedies passed down through generations. These would have included herbal remedies to treat colds, coughs, sprains, bruises, and other everyday issues. Scottish women who did healing among family were called the Cailleach-nan-Cearc (this translates to "hen wives") and were akin to the wise women found in many English villages. Quite a few of the Gaelic herbal spells and cures survive to this day, recorded for posterity by folklorists. Not certain is how old some of these traditions are, but many seem similar to those of an earlier time. However, you should even learn the more recent ones if they work.

One of the most popular healing techniques was eolas. This was a combination of an herbal concoction and a chant, prayer, or spell. This had to be sung or chanted over the herbs while they were being prepared or over the recipient while they were being healed. You can find many of these eolas spells in the Carmina Gadelica. Alexander Carmichael collected them on his travels in Victorian times throughout the Scottish Highlands and Islands

Ailein Dell, a blind poet, provides one of the best examples of an eolas chant. A Victorian writer called William Sharp recorded his spell under the name Fiona Mcleod, and it's used for curing an amadan, a simple-minded person or a madman. The original eolas contained a verse that invoked Christian figures, but it has been reworked slightly to be more Druid-friendly:

Deep peace I breathe into you,

O weariness, here:

O ache, here!

Deep peace, a soft white dove to you;

Deep peace, a quiet rain to you;

Deep peace, an ebbing wave to you!

Deep peace, red wind of the east from you;

Deep peace, grey wind of the west to you;

Deep peace, dark wind of the north from you;

Deep peace, blue wind of the south to you!

Deep peace, pure red of the flame to you;

Deep peace, pure white of the moon to you;

Deep peace, pure green of the grass to you;

Deep peace, pure brown of the earth to you;

Deep peace, pure grey of the dew to you,

Deep peace, pure blue of the sky to you!

Deep peace of the running wave to you,

Deep peace of the flowing air to you,

Deep peace of the quiet earth to you,

Deep peace of the sleeping stones to you!

Deep peace of the Yellow Shepherd to you,

Deep peace of the Wandering Shepherdess to you,

Deep peace of the Flock of Stars to you,

Deep peace of the Old Gods to you,

Deep peace of the Shining Ones to you.

The Beannachd na Cuairte is another popular healing practice. Translated as "blessing of the circle," it involves a large ring woven from healing plants, like woodbine. The patient would be passed through the ring, with his head and feet supported, typically three times. The ring would then be cut into nine bits, or it would be burned. Why nine? This number appears multiple times in Celtic mythology in different contexts. It also shows up in Norse mythology when a serpent that caused disease was chopped into nine, and the venom was used to create nine healing herbs. Egyptian mythology details an ancient papyrus that told how the serpent of chaos could be defeated. That papyrus covered nine chapters.

Other parts of the United Kingdom have similar ideas where a person with a disease would be passed through a ring – manmade or natural. In Cornwall, the Men-a-Tol stones have one large stone with a natural hole, big enough for a sick child to go through to be blessed by the stone.

There is a Welsh book called Physicians of the Myddfai, an herbal medicine book containing healing techniques a specific family of doctors passed down. These doctors served in the Myddfai region in Wales right back to the Middle Ages. They were Christians, and there are references to Christ, Mary, and the Saints in the book. Even though some of their ideas have a clear influence from Greek philosophy, many of the herbal recipes can easily be dated to pagan times. The book lists many diseases, along with the herbal remedies needed to treat them, and in Wales, one of the big botanical gardens is attempting to grow many of the herbs.

Let's take a quick look at nine of the herbs used for many centuries in Britain. Don't get too excited and go running out to find these herbs or any others for that matter. To understand herbal remedies, you have to understand the herbs. You must be able to distinguish between good and poisonous herbs, and you need to learn how to gather them properly (don't take the whole plant as the crop may not regrow.) Before you pick an herb, talk to it; they have a spirit too, and you can communicate with that spirit. Think about giving an offering in exchange for leaves or flowers because when a plant gives willingly, the potency is better.

- **Crios Cuchulainn** - Better known as meadowsweet (filipendula ulmaria), this is a stunning plant with white, delicate flowers that open in the springtime. The English name comes from its use in making mead a little sweeter, and when you brew mead for a ritual, you can still use it for this purpose. The Gaelic name tells us that the herb had an association with Cuchulainn, a warrior with a legend attached to him – whenever he was fevered, he would bathe in a meadowsweet bath. And before carpets became commonplace, meadowsweet would be scattered over the floor. As it was walked over, a pleasant aroma was released. Meadowsweet was also often used to treat an upset stomach.

- **Liath-lus** – Better known as mugwort (artemisia vulgaris), the Gaelic word translates to "the grey herb." It is still a popular herb to make into a tea to help facilitate lucid dreaming and clairvoyance. It was also used in stronger doses to treat worms, menstrual cramps, and constipation, and in medieval times travelers used it as a good luck charm.

- **Lus-na-fala** – Better known as yarrow (achillia millfolia). Before hops, yarrow was the popular choice for making good, strong beer. In medicinal terms, it was used for fevers and liver issues. It was also used to clean words and for treating cystitis.

- **Suibheag** – Better known as raspberry, (rubus idaeus) it is more than just a fruit we eat or make into a drink. The leaves are also used to make tea, often used for treating labor pains. However, it was not (and still isn't) recommended for women in early pregnancy. Strong doses were often given to those with diarrhea.

- **Athair an Talmhainn** - Better known as chamomile (anthemis nobilis). The leaves and the flower heads are still made into calming teas today and are also useful for insomnia. It is also used for upset stomachs and diarrhea and has long been used for indigestion.

- **Bainne bo Buidhe** - Better known as cowslip, the Gaelic word translates as "yellow milk cow." At one time, cowslip wine was one of the popular tonics. The flowers can be made into a sunburn balm; the flowers should be collected in the spring. Herbalists use the flowers for arthritis, and the root is good for bronchitis, whooping cough, and other similar conditions.

- **Bearnan Brighde** - Better known as dandelion (taraxacum officinalis) and the Gaelic word suggests an association with the Sant and the Goddess Brigid. It is mainly used as a diuretic, helping people urinate more and remove toxins from their systems quickly. It was also used to treat jaundice and other conditions affecting the liver; the leaves can be eaten in salads.

Questions to Consider

Before we look at the use of herbs, ask yourself these questions – they will help you get closer to herbs and understand them a little more: •

1. Have you ever used herbs before? For cooking? Perhaps in brewing or spells?

2. Have you ever tried communicating with plants? Ever felt any kind of presence from one?

3. Have you ever tried to be a vegetarian? Or changed your diet to include healthier foods? How did it make you feel?

Now try this:

If you don't have an herb garden already, go ahead and create one now. If you live in an apartment, you can use tubs or containers. If you have an herb garden already, try to create a healing concoction from edible herbs for you, a family member, and a pet. Do make sure nobody is allergic to the herbs before you start.

Plant Lore

As Britain used to be known, Merlin's Isle has a rich heritage in plant lore, one that can be traced back to the Bronze Age at the very least – that's at least 4000 years. From that heritage, we can tell you of thirteen ways plants can be used in Druidry:

1. **Food** – For the druids, it is a way of conveying Nwyfre, the Druid life force. Many traditions use wheat in a sacred way – Christianity, Eleusinian Mysteries, and at Lughnasadh (harvest time) by the pagans and the Druids. Another deeply symbolic food is the humble bean, especially with the Otherworld and the Ancestors. We all know how important the pig is in Celtic tradition, but if you study it beside the bean, you will see many similarities.

2. **In Drinks, Tonics, and Elixirs** – In the same way that plants can be used as food in ceremonies, so can sacred drinks. Druid rituals usually include mead – usually made from heather pollinated by bees; heather is closely associated with community and joy. Several elixirs made from birch sap or dandelion and burdock, to name a couple, allow Druids to have enhanced health and a better connection to the past.

3. **As Clothing** – Modern druids know of how clothes – or not wearing any at all – can enhance a ritual. For many thousands of years, the main clothing was linen made out of flax, and the result is these tiny little seeds are responsible for civilization advancing so well. Our ancestors also used plants like Weld and Woad to dye cloth, and these are used to this day to dye the clothing we wear at our rituals.

4. **For Consciousness Journeys** – Some plants have a psychotropic effect on our consciousness, but this is nothing new since this has been well documented in contemporary and ancient indigenous traditions. We have no proof this ever happened in Druidry or any other ancient Celtic culture, even though the Psylocibin mushroom (Liberty Cap) and the Fly Agaric mushroom were prevalent. Still, there is the suggestion that some herbs, like mugwort, were smoked as a way of stimulating psychic powers. Not so long ago, a 1ˢᵗ Century Druid was unearthed near Colchester, and mugwort was found on the drinking cup with him. It seems that, for sensible reasons, modern druids should follow this and drink mugwort rather than smoking it.

5. **Medicinal Use** – Herbalism has one of the oldest histories, but classical writers recorded just four plants used by Druids for medicinal and magical purposes – vervain, mistletoe, samolus (likely Water Pimpernel), and selago (Fir Club moss). However, with a correlation of the archaeobotanical records detailing the plants growing when the Ancient Druids were around in western Europe and writing from herbalists like Dioscorides, together with Old Celtic references, we do know what plants would have been used, like valerian.

6. **For Anointing** – An example would be vervain or oils of primrose because some old texts mention being part of Ceridwen's brew, which was used for blessing bards.

7. **In Rituals** – Druid ceremonies often include flowers, and the Druid Samhain ritual uses garlic. Before a ritual feast can be partaken, the Spirits of the Departed are invited in. But the sprinkling of cloves across the threshold precedes this. Also, flower petals are often used in circle casting Beltane and other festivities.

8. **In Incense** – Druids often use incense to perfume and cleanse an aura or working space. Two of the best herbs are juniper berries and agrimony.

9. **In Lustrations** – Ritual washing of the face, hands, body, tools, altar, circle, or anything used in a ritual can be made better when you add certain plants to the water. Agrimony is a good one; its Gaelic name is Mur-druidhean, which translates to "the sorrow of the Druids" but actually means "the dispeller of sorrow used by the Druids."

10. **In Spells** -Druids are cautious when it comes to spells because they understand the meaning behind the saying, "When the Gods want to punish us, they answer our prayers." Ancient druids used spell work, and sometimes contemporary Druids might, but only after considering the magical and ethical implications. Many centuries ago, fern was used for invisibility. Modern Druid spells may still use it; not for true invisibility, obviously, but if they wanted to pass unnoticed somewhere.

11. **In Talismans and Charms** – Those that follow the Old Ways are already familiar with vibrations and energy. Plants emanate vibrations, and carrying a bit of that plant around with us exerts influence over our aura. One of those is betony since it has tons of beneficial properties and was once known as the "cure-all." Mandrake was another traditional and highly renowned plant in Ancient Times, and it's almost certain it was taken into Britain in the earliest days.

12. **As Offerings** – Gift giving is an innate part of humankind, and it makes sense to offer flowers to a couple getting married, to a deity on an altar, or on the grave of a loved one at a funeral. Our ancestors used Meadowsweet and Vervain in their offerings.

13. **For Oracular Use** - Plant parts, like yarrow stalks (in China and Celtic lands), are used for divination. Others, especially those with psychotropic properties, are used to access our oracular consciousness powers. The Druid Plant Oracle translates the traditional plant meaning (of those used by the Druids) into contemporary terms that match what we face in today's world.

Chapter 7: The Tree Alphabet

Images from https://darachcroft.com/

Ogham (pronounced as OH-am, with a silent g) is one of the most ancient alphabets, used in Old Irish, Pictish, Welsh, and other Brittonic languages. It can be dated to about the 3rd century CE and is sometimes known as the Celtic Tree Alphabet. That's because each letter is given a plant or tree name, but this is likely to have happened after the alphabet was created.

The Ogham alphabet was sidelined in favor of the Roman Alphabet for writing Old Irish after the 6th century CE, but a book written in the 14th century called the Book of Ballymote (or *Leabhar Bhaile an Mhóta)* contains plenty of mythologies, genealogies, and Irish history, all written in the Ogham script.

The book also has older manuscripts with Ogham scripts, including The Scholars Primer from the 7th century (*Auraicept na n-Éces*) and The Book of the Taking of Ireland from the 11th century (*Lebor Gabála Érenn*). The 14th-century document titled In Lebor Ogaim, or The Ogham Tract or The Book of Ogams, also contains detailed Ogham descriptions.

Some of these manuscripts contain descriptions detailing the Ogham alphabet's invention by Fenius, the Scythian King, after the Tower of Babel. But, the Ogam Tract disagrees, stating that Ogma (also known as Oghma or Ogmios), the Irish God of writing and communication, actually created it.

Throughout locations in western Britain and Ireland, many Ogham inscriptions have been found. The most ancient ones are found on stone slabs, detailing personal names, and were typically seen as memorials or territorial markers. They may also have been inscribed on trees, stakes, and sticks.

The original Ogham alphabet contained 20 characters or feda, which were placed into four groups or aicmi. Each aicme contained five characters and was named for its first letter:

Aicme Beithe - "the B Group"

Aicme hÚatha - "the H Group"

Aicme Muine - "the M Group"

Aicme Ailme - "the A Group"

After the 6th century, a fifth group was added, likely because the Irish language changed.

Typically, the alphabet is written bottom to top vertically, but horizontal script written left to right has also been found, although this is usually in manuscripts. The letters are linked with one solid line, as you will see later. First, though, Robert Graves wrote a book called The White Goddess in which he talks about the alphabet being related to Celtic religious ceremonies and beliefs. He also said that the order of the alphabet letters for a tree magic calendar, each letter corresponding to a specific Celtic month:

Beith – Birch - December 24th – January 20th

Luis – Rowan– January 21st - February 17th

Nion - Ash - February 18th - March 17th

Fearn – Alder - March 18th - April 14th

Saille – Willow - April 15th - May 12th

Uath - Hawthorn - May 13th - June 9th

Duir - Oak - June 10th - July 7th

Tinne – Holly - July 8th - August 4th

Coll – Hazel - August 5th - September 1st

Muin – Vine - September 2nd to September 29th

Gort – Ivy - September 30th - October 27th

Ngetal – Reed - October 28th - November 24th

Ruis – Elder - November 25th - December 22nd

You might note from these dates there isn't a tree for December 23rd. That is because it is the "Year and a Day" traditional day in the early law courts.

The Tree Alphabet

The rest of this chapter is devoted to the alphabet's actual letters and what they mean in terms of the trees they are associated with. The image of each letter shows you clearly how to write it too, so study these and get practicing – soon, you can create cryptic garden books, have cryptic tattoos, and anything else you want using these letters.

A is for Ailm (A-lum)

Primary association – the elm

Secondary associations – pine and fir

The trees associated with this letter are tall and straight, indicating height and perspective. Ancient Celtic lore says that the elm is bound intimately with death and transitioning to the underworld and the fir trees with inner soul healing. The Wych elm is the most grown in Scotland, but contrary to popular belief, it has nothing to do with witches. Instead, it references the elm's flexibility, and the name comes from a verb in Old English, which means "to give way." Elm is not the best wood to construct buildings from, but its flexibility and ability to withstand water make it good for wheels, bridges, and boat hulls, not to mention coffins. The Welsh also made their longbows from elm, while the English used yew.

B is for BEITH ('BAE-yh')

Primary association – the birch, especially the silver birch

Celtic mythology called the birch tree "The Lady of the Woods." It represents change, purification, new beginnings, family connections, healing, protection, grace, femininity, purity, rebirth, and new life. This should be obvious, given that the birch comes into leaf earlier than many others in the spring. It is also called the "pioneer tree" because, after a natural disaster, it can re-colonize the woodlands. Scottish Highland folklore says that if a birch stick were used to herd a barren cow, it would become fertile.

The wood from a birch tree is tough, straight-grained, and heavy and was typically used for making furniture, while the bark was used for tanning leather.

C is for COLL ('Col')

Primary association – the hazel

Celtic mythology says that hazel is associated with knowledge, creativity, and wisdom. It is one of the oldest native British trees, with traces of shells and pollen going back around 10,000 years. To this day, the straight shoots that come up from the tree's base are used as walking sticks or pinned to grow into shepherd's crooks. English pilgrims used hazel to make staffs for walking sticks and self-defense. In medieval times, it was used for weaving baskets.

D is for DAIR OR DUIR ('Dahr')

Primary association – the oak

Celtic lore and mythology associates the oak with self-confidence, resilience, and strength and is one of the best trees for inner strength enhancement, specifically in times of loss. The Gaelic word "duir" means durable, and oak wood has long been valued for its durability and strength, especially in construction, while the bark was used for tanning.

E is for EADHA ('EH-ga')

Primary association – the aspen

Aspen has long been associated with courage, endurance, and overcoming obstacles. In the Scottish Highlands, there were rumors that the aspen had a connection to the Fairy Realm. Also, in the Highlands, they had a tradition whereby the aspen wouldn't be used to construct houses, agricultural tools, or fishing implements, suggesting that the aspen was seen as a fairy tree, much like the rowan tree was.

However, when dry, aspen is light and buoyant and was always a good choice for paddles and oars, and armor and shields, given its highly protective abilities. Celtic mythology saw the aspen as spiritually protective. Because the leaf is unique in shape, it whispers in the wind, and the Celts believed this was a form of communication from their ancestors.

F is for FEÀRN ('Fyaarn')
Primary association – the alder

Celtic mythology associates the alder with secrecy, water, bad luck, nature, balance, and spirituality. These trees were mysterious to the Celts since, when the sap is exposed to the air, it turns deep red. This made the Celts think the trees would bleed when they were cut.

Irish Mythology tells us of Deirdre of the Sorrows fleeing to Alba with the son of Usna, Naoise. She wanted to get away from Conchobhar mac Nessa, the King of Ireland, whom Dierdre was meant to marry. The couple hid in the alder woods in Glen Etive, contributing something towards the Celtic lore themes of secrecy and hiding.

Alder wood is oily. It turns hard when submerged in water and was often used to construct water pipes, buckets, bridge foundations, and other similar constructions. Like the birch, the alder is also a "pioneer tree" because it can heal woodlands and landscapes destroyed by cutting, storms, floods, fire, and more. The flowers can produce a green dye that used to be used for camouflaging clothing (think Robin Hood) and concealing fairies from the human eye.

G is for GORT ('GOR-ht')

Primary association – the ivy

Celtic mythology often associated ivy with growth, prosperity, and good fortune, especially for women. It was thought that if you allowed it to grow up your house walls, it would protect all inhabitants from curses and magic, but if it fell or died, misfortune would rain down on the house. The Druids related ivy with peace because of its ability to wind around different plant species, binding them. Young women often carried a piece of ivy for fertility and food luck, and today it is often seen at weddings as a symbol of fidelity.

H is for HUATH ('HOO-er')

Primary association – the hawthorn

Celtic mythology associates the hawthorn with defense, protection, and cleansing. However, if the hawthorn stem is brought into a house, it is said to bring about bad luck, likely because many hawthorn species smell of decay and death when cut.

The hawthorn tree is sometimes called the Fairy Tree and is said to stand guard outside the fairy's realm entrance. Thomas the Rhymer, a Scottish poet and mystic, and the Fairy Queen were said to have met under the hawthorn tree. When Rhymer returned from the realm, he discovered he had been away for seven years.

Celtic mythology also tells us that the Fairies inhabited the hawthorn trees, and if these trees were damaged or cut down, it would bring about the wrath of the tree's supernatural guardians. Fairies were not considered friendly creatures as we depict them today; they were respected and feared, surrounded by tales of curses and kidnapping, and the hawthorn tree was often revered and respected.

I is for IOGH ('Yoo')

Primary association – the yew

The yew tree is a Celtic symbol of death and resurrection, possibly because the branches that droop down and touch the ground can take root and grow new trees. It may also be because there is no medicinal value to the yew, and most, if not all, is poisonous to animals and humans. Yet, the yew tree can live for thousands of years and is often seen in graveyards or places with a spiritual significance that came before the Christians. One of the oldest yew trees in Britain, possibly in Europe, is called the Fortingall Yew growing in Perthshire, and it is thought to be at least 2-3000 years old.

Yew wood is hard and close-grained, and it is long known, not just for making furniture but also for making the English Longbow. Scots would also use yew for their longbows, and some say that Robert the Bruce ordered longbows to be made from the Ardchattan Priory's sacred yews – these were used at Bannockburn in 1314.

L is for LUIS ('LOO-sh')

Primary association – the rowan

The rowan tree is also called the Mountain Ash and is associated with life, perseverance, humanity, insight, blessings, and protection against magic and enchantments. The Celtic Druids believed that women came from the rowan tree, and as such, it is a symbol of motherhood, life fragility, protection, blood, birth, and survival.

Rowan trees are quite small and are usually found on their own. They are common trees in the Scottish Highlands because they can grow at higher altitudes and in shallow soil, where few other trees survive. The Celts believed that the mountaintops were where the veil between the mortal world and the heavens was thin, possibly explaining why Celtic mythology holds the rowan as spiritually significant.

Rowan wood is resilient and is often used for walking sticks, spinning wheels, spindles, and tool handles. Many believe that cutting a rowan tree down will bring bad luck.

M is for MUIN ('MOO-n')

Primary association – the vine
Secondary association – the bramble

Muin symbolizes life's lessons learned and inward journeys. There is some argument over whether the primary association with the vine is correct. Although it featured heavily in Bronze Age art, it didn't arrive in Britain until 2000 years ago, when the Romans introduced wine. But the bramble is a winding plant that bears fruit like the vine and is native to cooler climates, like northern Europe. The Gaelic word for bramble is Dris-Muine, translating to "prickle thorn," which supports the theory.

The vine symbolizes wrath and happiness, with a connection to truthful speaking and prophecy. Apparently, the bramble is associated with the devil, and Celts refused to eat blackberries, as they believed the devil had spat on them. This satanic association continues into Christian mythology; it was believed that when Satan was kicked out of heaven, he landed in a bramble patch, cursing them as they pricked him. Goats are some of the few animals that will eat brambles, and we all know they have a Christian association with the devil.

N is for NUIN ('NOO-n')

Primary association – the ash

The ash has long symbolized divination, wisdom, and knowledge. Celtic druids believed men came from the ash tree, leading to its association with rebirth, masculinity, and strength. Several legends connect the ash with the Gods, and it is considered a sacred tree. Norse legend tells of Yggdrasil, the World Tree thought to be an ash that reached its roots deep into the underworld and its trunk to heaven. Odin, a well-known Norse God, received wisdom and insight after hanging from the tree for nine days.

Historically, ash is thought to have protective and healing properties. British folklore tells us that, to protect them from being taken by changeling fairies, newborns were given ash sap, and ash berries were put in their cradles.

Ash is good weight-bearing wood and was used for building stagecoach axles. Before that, it was used to make spear shafts and bows too, where yew was unavailable.

O is for ONN ('OH-n')

Primary association – the gorse

Celtic mythology tells us that gorse protected against spiteful fairies and misfortune and is associated with optimism and resilience, the light, the Sun, and fire. Gorse is always looking for the light and warmth and will quickly sprout shoots. Even today, a controlled burn is used to clear it, encouraging new shoots to come through. In terms of protection against the fairies, folklore tells us it could be achieved if gorse branches surrounded the bed.

Gorse wood will burn fiercely and at high temperatures and can be used as a fuel source. It has bright yellow flowers, which make a yellow dye for clothes. The flowers are typically found between January and June.

P is for PEITH BHOG ('Payh fvog')

Primary association – downy birch

The same as Beith, the birch stood for purity, love, and birth and was often hung over cradles to protect babies from evil spirits. Burch twig bundles were also used to drive the old year's spirits out.

Downy birch differs from silver birch – it is more upright, and the bark is browner with horizontal grooves and not so papery as the silver. Downy birch can be found further west and north and often grows at elevations few trees can withstand. The sap was used to make ale, wine, and drinks in the spring.

R is for RUIS ('Roosh')

Primary association – the elder

The elder is associated with endings, maturity, and transitions. Both Celtic and British folklore tells us that the elder was used to protect against evil fairies, the devil, and witches. If elder was burned, the devil would show himself, but if elder was planted beside your house, the devil would stay away. Traditionally, the best protection is considered to be a rowan tree planted at the front door and an elder tree at the back door.

Elder is a hardwood and off-white, and it is a good carving and whittling wood when mature. The smaller stems were hollowed out to make beads, musical instruments, and other small craft items. Apparently, fairy folk love merrymaking and music, mostly from instruments crafted of elder wood. Foliage was used to keep flies at bay, and branches would be hung in dairies to stop milk from going sour.

Elder flowers are commonly used in wine, cordial, and tea, and while it isn't a common Scottish tree, much of the elder was used in the Harris Tweed industry for dying. Green and yellow dyes came from the leaves, purple and blue from the berries, and black and grey from the bark.

S is for SUIL ('Sool')

Primary association – the willow

Celtic lore and culture tell us that the willow was associated with spiritual growth, adaptability, optimism, and knowledge. They are easy to grow; simply pushing a living branch into the ground can quickly result in a new tree. In some parts of the world, this symbolizes immortality, vitality, renewal, and growth.

The willow was important in Celtic mythology, considered sacred because they are mostly found by lochs and riverbanks – both are spiritually significant. Celts also considered borders important, with the rowan sacred as a border between heaven and Earth and the willow as a border between eater and land.

In some cultures, the willow was associated with mourning and sadness, but Celtic culture saw the willow as relocating itself after nature or man uprooted it.

Willows are also Pioneer trees, spreading their roots to stop riverbanks from eroding. The wood is used for basket weaving, wickerwork, cricket stumps, and cricket bats. In the 19th century, scientists found salicylic acid in willow, similar to aspirin's primary ingredient.

T is for TEINE ('TEEN-uh')

Primary association – the holly

The evergreen holly was associated with immortality, regeneration, and fertility, and it was said to be bad luck to cut down an entire tree. However, holly sprigs are often used for decoration, and it used to be used to protect homes from evil fairies or to let them shelter with humans in a frictionless way. Some also said that if a holly tree were grown close to a house, it would protect it from lightning strikes.

Folklore has holly as the King of the Woods from the summer to the winter solstice. The Oak King would then defeat holly, and he would rule until the next summer solstice. Holly was seen as oak's rival for the Lady of the Woods, birch, who switched from oak to holly and then back.

These days, full-grown holly trees are rare, and they are often found growing in hedgerows or as part of a beech or oak wood. The wood has been used to make furniture and walking sticks, due to it being a heavy hardwood.

U is for UR ('OohS')

Primary association – the heather

Heather is a symbol of generosity, passion, healing, and luck. Its flowers are attractive to bees, and they are seen as messengers between the mortal realm and the spirit world. The heather and the thistle compete in Scotland to be the most iconic plant. Here, heather is akin to the four-leafed clover, but taking it indoors is considered unlucky unless it was to protect against witches. Fairy Folk are said to live in heather bells and feast on heather honey.

The Celts talked of heather as a plant of romance, attraction, and intoxication. It was used to make mead and ale but was also used to thatch roofs, make brooms, dyes, baskets, and more. According to folklore, the Picts made ale just from heather, without adding hops, malt, or anything else.

Chapter 8: Druidry and Divination

Ancient Druids practiced many divination methods, from watching to weather to interpreting bird flight, observing how animals behave, and interpreting planetary configurations. It's almost certain that all four elements were used the same as they were for healing, and it is highly likely that Earth's conveyed signs and feelings were cast on drum skins or sheets and read in the same way fortune tellers read tea-leaves. It's also thought they found inspiration in images they saw in the fire or clouds passing above them, even in water pools. The Irish Druids called cloud divination "Neldoracht," and we also know that they had other, more complex divination methods, such as "Tarbhfeis," when the diviner believed being wrapped in the hide of a bull helped their clairvoyance.

You don't have to think about divination as being nothing more than fortune-telling. In fact, it is one of the most effective ways of unearthing hidden dynamics, be they within you, a group, or a relationship. In that way, divination becomes a way of gaining knowledge about yourself and understanding more deeply what causes appearance. It becomes a way of going beneath the surface, paying more attention to cause than effect.

What does this mean for modern-day Druids? Well, they can use this with several divination methods very distinctly Druidic. That includes working with the sacred plants and animals from Druid and Celtic tradition and with Ogham, which is the Druidic tree alphabet we talked about in the previous chapter. Allegedly, the Druids made use of Ogham in their divination. Many stories from the Medieval Irish, including the Tochmarc Etaine, tell us this was likely, although there have been Ogham inscriptions found on stones that only date to the fourth or fifth century. We can't be sure that the Druids used Ogham, but it gives us a way of understanding future events and hidden dynamics. Plus, today, it is an integral part of Druid training.

The remainder of this chapter will discuss intention manifestation and rituals.

Simple Intention Manifestation

Before you can even think about rituals or anything else, you need to set your intention. This type of manifestation is quite simple and involves three steps:

1. **Make Sure You Really Want What You Are Asking For.** You need not detail everything, and you don't even need a picture in your head. You do need a desire - simple, clear, positive, and with no doubts. This isn't always easy because you may have doubts you didn't realize you had.

2. **Be Realistic in Your Belief That it Can Happen.** This isn't always easy, and it does depend on what you want to manifest and your faith level. It's simple, though - if you don't believe it will happen, it won't. For that reason, beginners should start with more believable things.

3. **Make Yourself Believe That it Will Happen.** Wrap yourself in happiness and gratitude. Many find it helpful to say, out loud or to yourself, "I am grateful that X is going to happen." Repeat it or something similar a couple of times, and imagine

how it would feel when it happens. It won't take long before you start to feel it, and then you can just watch it happen.

Ritual Goals and Life Circumstances

One thing that can help you establish a daily ritual is thinking hard and seriously about the practice before you start. Don't do a daily ritual just because someone else says you should. Do them for your own reasons; do them to enrich your life; do them to bring about connection and grounding. Your motivation must be intrinsic, even if a Druid order told you you should do it, and you must be motivated by the fact that you want to do them, not that you should do them. These questions can help you find your motivation and work out what you want from the practice.

1. What Do You Want to Accomplish During Your Day?

If you can articulate your goals, you stand a better chance of deciding the most appropriate practices. Ideas include:

- Devotion or prayer
- A connection with nature
- Improving your clarity and mental health
- Deeper spiritual practice
- Starting the day positively or in a sacred way
- Ending the day positively or in a sacred way
- Preparing yourself for sacred living and/or dreaming
- A daily commitment
- Taking a moment out of a tough day
- Just feeling good about life and yourself

Draw up a list of what you want to achieve and take it from there.

2. Do You Belong to an Order or Tradition? Do They Offer Daily Practice or Rituals?

If the answer to both of those is yes, then that's great. Most orders or traditions have a daily practice, be it a prayer, a meditation, or an energy working. This does two things – connects you to your tradition and lets you focus in useful ways.

3. How Much Time Do You Want to Spend on Your Ritual?

How much time do you have spare? 5 minutes a day? 15? More? You should have a basic practice that can be done wherever you are, be it at work, at home, traveling somewhere, or whatever. You should also have another practice, an extended one you can do once or twice a week.

Remember that this is the long haul. Start small, with something sustainable and not with something that you have no way of sustaining over the long-term. When you start small and get the results you want, you can add more in good time. When you start big and struggle to maintain your daily practice, you will feel bad, and your spiritual growth will suffer.

4. What Time of Day Suits You Best?

You must fit your daily practice into your day, so it works and at a time that works. If you end your workday exhausted, you will get nowhere if you try to do a 15-minute meditation – you'll just fall asleep. A better way would be to do it at lunchtime or in the morning, even when taking a bath. Test different times of the day and see what works best for you.

5. Can Your Existing Routines Be Altered or Extended?

Think about what you are doing already. Can this be extended or altered into daily practice? For instance, let's say that you live on a homestead, and your job is to take care of the animal chores for about half an hour each morning. These chores must be done, regardless of weather, so that is a great time to do your daily practice, without having to make a special time or change your routine in any way.

Test and Form Habits

So, by now, you should have drawn up a plan that works for your daily practice. Now you need to test it. Why? Because your plan may look great on paper, but it might not work. Lots of new druids have all the right enthusiasm, but they get so excited that they draw up a plan with so many practices it cannot be sustained over the long term. It's best to start with one small practice you can easily commit to that's just 5 minutes or maybe 10 minutes a day. So, testing your practice will help you get it right, not just the timing but also the practices themselves.

Try your practice for one lunar cycle. That gives you plenty of time to get into it, to see what works and what doesn't. If something doesn't work, swap it out or another practice or remove it altogether. Keep going until you get the right combination of practices – take the time and have the patience to see it through to reap the rewards.

When you are happy with your practice, you need to work at making it a habit. Habits are formed when you do something repeatedly for long enough. For example, brushing your teeth in the morning and at night. You don't think about doing it; you just do it. Habits typically take from as little as 15 days to over 200 days to form, depending on what the habit is and your personal circumstances.

You also need to realize something else very important – when your life circumstances undergo a major change, you may need to change your daily practices. There's nothing wrong with that, and it could be for any reason – a baby, a new job, a new relationship, a new home, or anything. Whatever it is, you will need to re-evaluate your practice, when, and how you do it. It must work for you, not against you.

Last, you must be flexible. Let's say you like to go for a long walk first thing in the morning, and that's where you do your practice. If it's pouring rain, you need to switch to having a cup of tea on your porch and still do your practice. Making changes is fine, so long as they benefit you.

Examples of Daily Practices and Rituals

You can do loads of rituals, and I'll give you a few ideas that can help kick-start your own ideas. Remember that these need not be formal. You can spend quiet time outdoors in nature or drink a cup of tea in the moonlight, basically anything that benefits your spiritual practice.

• Daily Altar Work and Prayers

These are likely what most people think daily ritual work is all about. You can treat your altar as your center for your spiritual practice, and your focus for all that you do can be based around this, tending to it every day and spending time there. Think about any or all of these:

> • Leaving an offering for the deity, guides, or spirit each day. You could offer spring water one day and then a plant the second day.

> • Burn candles or incense for a short period

> • Do a tarot card draw or daily divination

> • Speak affirmations or offer prayers, such as the Druid's Prayer or write your prayers

> • Do a short meditation

> • Do daily ritual work

Altar work goes a long way towards evolving you, changing as you change in your journey or as your circumstances change and when your circumstances change.

• Greet the Sun

It doesn't matter whether you get up as dawn breaks or at a later time; one of the best practices you can do is greet the Sun and honor it. This is nothing more than a minute out of your day, but it is one of the most powerful ways to connect yourself with our beautiful planet's life-giver. A simple greeting involves facing east, raising your arms, and feeling the Sun's rays on you. Observe the rays hitting the landscape and the leaves on the trees. If the clouds and/or rain obscure the Sun, you can still do this. Face east and raise your arms to the clouds. Thank the spirits for sending the rain. After both greetings, lower your arms, bow your head, cross your arms, and chant an "Awen" as often as you need to get daily inspiration.

• Commune with the Moon

The moon's phases are another great opportunity, and you can make or buy a moon calendar. You may not always see the moonrise; the weather may be bad, or the time may not fit in with your day. But you can still acknowledge the moon. Brew yourself a cup of tea using lunar herbs – clary sage, passionflower, mugwort, violet, ginger, hibiscus, etc. Take it outside, unless it is freezing, in which case stand or sit near a window. Hold the tea, so the moon reflects in it. Stay like that for a couple of minutes, and then drink the tea. Keep a little in the cup as an offering, pouring it out onto the earth.

• Tree Energy Exchange

Find a large tree you can easily get to and stand with your back placed against it. Allow the tree's energy to flow into you, especially when your energy is depleted and you are exhausted. If the opposite is true and you have too much energy, face the tree, press your front against it, and let the energy flow into the tree.

• Eat Mindfully and Honor the Harvest

Consider this for at least one of your daily meals as it helps connect you to the Earth, having gratitude for all that it offers. Make it a meal you eat alone or can be in silence for (remember you may not get that opportunity every day) and take your meal somewhere nice, where you can observe the land and take in the Sun. Put your hands over your meal, and use your own words to give gratitude for it. It could be to the land, the farmers, those involved in preparing and shipping the food, etc. It works even better if you grew the food and prepared the meal yourself. Be present with the meal by enjoying every mouthful, chewing it, tasting it, and engaging with all of your senses. When your meal is done, don't forget to offer gratitude.

• Daily Divination

This can give you a great deal of insight into your day, give you ideas for meditation themes, and is a great way of learning divination. You do it with an ogham, oracle, or tarot deck, and a one-card draw or a simple stave draw every day is a great way of starting or ending the day. You can also combine this with many practices.

• Candle Meditation

Candle meditation encourages rest and calm and helps cultivate your inner vision and strengthen your focus. The best time to do this is just before bedtime. To take part in vivid dreaming:

1. Burn a little mugwort at the same time. The room should be dark; light the candle and put it in front of you.

2. Stare at it, getting an image of it fixed in your mind.

3. As you do so, allow your breath to get quiet and get into a comfortable position.

4. Once you feel calm, shut your eyes, but maintain a vision of the burning flame in your mind's eye.

5. Breathe steadily, focusing on the flame. If your focus goes, open your eyes, get the image of the flame back in your mind, and shut them again.

Doing this for just five minutes every day can yield amazing results.

Chapter 9: Ogham Divination

The Celts created the Ogham alphabet. The credit, courtesy of Irish legend, actually goes to Ogma, the Celtic God of learning, wisdom, and eloquence, along with credit for gifting the alphabet to humanity. Although the Ogham is a very old alphabet, we have no tangible evidence that it came before Christianity. Stones found with Ogham carvings have been dated as far back as 300 to 700 CE.

According to Catherine Swift or History today:

"Dating ogham is difficult and often problematic: although the alphabet itself was created rather earlier, the evidence suggests that the surviving inscriptions of ogham in Ireland belong predominantly to the fifth and sixth centuries... Ogham was developed during the Roman Empire and demonstrates the spread of its influence far beyond the imperial frontiers; the fact that ogham has five vowel symbols (although Gaelic has ten such sounds) is one of the reasons scholars believe that the Latin alphabet, which also uses five vowels, was an influence on the invention of the system. Ogham was not a single, fixed system and the surviving stones show modifications, as new symbols were invented and older ones were lost."

Originally, the alphabet looks to have been used for boring purposes, such as identifying property lines or gravestone markings. Each letter in the alphabet is called a "few" and is identified by a plant or tree (see chapter 7) regarded as sacred by the Celts. Originally, there were only 20 letters, but five more were added although, so little can be found about the additional letters that most users stick to the original ones.

While we cannot prove definitively that Ancient Druids used the Ogham for divination, an Irish epic published in the ninth century called The Wooing of Etain contains a scene where Dallan, a Druid, used the fews to discover where Midir hid Etain.

The Ogham showed up again in a classic from the early 20th century, Robert Graves' The White Goddess. At least two chapters were dedicated to Ogham folklore, but critics dismissed it as nothing more than poetic speculation rather than historical fact we can rely on. However, that brought attention back to the Ogham and was partly responsible for Modern Paganism, especially Wicca and Goddess spirituality. If you can get hold of a copy, it is worth reading.

Ogham Staves

Ogham divination is traditionally done using staves, although you can use pieces of paper if you need to do a divination ritual quickly. Making your own staves is simple. You will need 25 twigs or sticks roughly the same length – 26 if you want a blank stave. If you can't find enough sticks the same length, use dowel rods, all cut to about 4-6 inches.

Sand the sticks so all the bark is off, and they are smooth. Each stick needs to be inscribed with a different Ogham symbol – this can be carved, painted, or you can use a wood-burning tool.

As you make your staves, take time to think about what each symbol means. As you carve, paint or burn them into the wood, think about them, feel them and feel each symbol's magical energy embedding itself into the stake. Creation is a magical act, so it works best to make your staves within a magical space. If your altar setup doesn't allow you to use a wood-burning pen, use another method, or find a suitable workspace you can transform into a temporary altar. Hold each individual stave before you inscribe, and afterward, take the time to fill it with your energy and power. And when finished, your staves must be consecrated before their first use, in the same way as you would with any magical tool.

Reading staves for Ogham divination can be done in several ways, and it's up to you to work out which way works best for you. Some people prefer to carry their staves in a pouch with them so that, when a question needs an answer, they can pull out the required number of staves to answer that question. Three is one of the best numbers, but you can use as many as you want. For each stave you draw out, determine its meaning in divination terms, using the following guide.

Ogham Few Meanings

In terms of divination, the symbols you carve into the wood are as follows. The fews or letters are divided into four groups or aicmes.

First Aicme - the Beith Aicme
The Birch-Beith (Beh or be-yeh)

This represents new starts and beginnings. Drawing this may indicate a figurative or literal house cleaning is required as it is associated with purification, cleansing, removing clutter, and childbirth (new beginnings).

The Rowan-Luis (lweesh or loo-sh)

This represents protection against physical, spiritual and magical danger, sanctuary, defense, and control of your senses.

The Alder-Fern (fair-n or fyarn)

This represents inspiration, prophecy, and protection you get after following good advice. It also represents you laying foundations to achieve your goals.

Willow-Saille (sahl-yuh or sal-ye)

This represents intuition, feelings, flexibility, dreams, imagination, lunar rhythms, and feminine principle. But it is also a warning against deception.

Ash-Nuin (nee-un or nyin)

This represents growth, change, fate, transformation, destiny, possibilities, options, potential, and the whole reality. If you draw this stave, be prepared to walk the walk and talk the talk.

Second Aicme - the Huathe Aicme

Hawthorn-Huathe (hoo-ah or OOa-huh)

This represents complications, obstacles, prickly situations, and drawing. It could tell you to clean your act up, show discipline and restraint, and persist, but be careful.

Oak-Duir (doo-r or doo-er)

This represents endurance, strength, strong foundations, strong vocations, and support and protection in all you pursue. It could be telling you to rely on your strengths.

Holly-Tinne (chin-yuh or tying-yuh)

This represents testing, challenges, trials, strengthening, and tempering and could indicate that you need to be prepared to defend yourself and your position.

Hazel-Coll (cull or coll)

This represents knowledge, wisdom, inspiration, enlightenment, and divinatory or poetic gifts. It could be telling you to use meditation or inner guidance to seek knowledge.

Quert-Apple (kwairt or kyert)

This represents health, recuperation, vitality, or respite, and choosing between two great alternatives. The message is to choose carefully and wisely.

Third Aicme - the Muin Aicme

Vine-Muin (muhn or min-ye)

This represents loose inhibitions, intoxication, and the resulting truth. It also represents the completion of harvest or work and celebration. It could be telling you to speak your mind, or it may be warning you to watch what you say.

Ivy-Gort

This represents survival, tenacity, growth, ruthlessness, restriction, ill treatment, exploitation, busting barriers down, or surviving in tough conditions. It could be telling you to be persistent and learn to survive and thrive no matter what.

Reed-NgEtal (nyeh-tl or nyay-tl)

This represents purging, cleansing, healing, medicine, and removing negativity. It could be telling you you need to do a cleansing, that you need to work out where the trouble is brewing, and work for reconciliation and unity afterward.

Blackthorn-Straif (strahf or straf)

This represents adversity, strife, physical or emotional damage, or it could even mean you have only unpleasant choices to make. It could be telling you that you need to take charge of your own destiny and choose the best from all the available options.

Elder-Ruis (rweesh or reesh)

This represents anger, shame, humiliation, regret, and karma. It also represents endings and new beginnings, and it could be telling you to go with the flow, put the worst behind you, do better in the future, and move on with your head held up.

Fourth Aicme - the Ailim Aicme

Silver Fir – Ailim (ahlm or al yem)

This represents a better perspective and more consciousness, wonder, elevation, enthusiasm, pain, fear, and awe. It could be telling you that you need to look at the bigger picture.

Gorse-Ohn (uhn or on)

This represents value and sweetness gathering together and things that come together in your favor. It also represents sexuality, attraction, sensuality, vitality, health, and passion. It could be telling you that you should be grateful and share the good things coming to you.

Heather-Ur (oor)

This represents maturity and consummation in a relationship, acceptance of your shadow side, conquering it, and homemaking. The message could be to open up, be more realistic in your love ideals, accept your shadow side, and make peace with it.

Aspen-Eadha (eh-yuh or ayda)

This represents doubt, fear, long odds, beating those odds, rites of passage, and testing. It also represents resolution, warrior spirit, courage, and confidence. It could be telling you to take hold of your courage, overcome the obstacles in your way, and you could end up beating the odds.

Yew-Ioho (ee-yoh or yoho)

This represents endings, death, transition, change, and exits. Although something may be dying, it will be followed by renewal or a re-birth. The advice is to embrace the change. Understand that dying is a natural part of life, be it a person, relationship, or anything else. Understand that all endings come with a new beginning.

Basic Meditation Rituals Using Ogham Tree Lore

The following technique is based on tree lore:

Tools

• Wands – Yes, more than one! You need a series of wands made from the wood of the Ogham alphabet trees. You need up to seven – the Four directions and the rest for the Circle.

• Candles – at least one, a large candle to use in the Circle

• Incense

• A small chalice or a goblet – glass, ceramic, pewter, whatever you use in your rituals

• Mead, ale, malt whiskey, or wine

• Any object you want as a focus. This can be a picture, a feather, a crystal, or whatever suits the ritual.

• A portable altar or small table

• Cushion or chair

• Athame – this is optional, depends on your tradition

• Drum – optional, depends on the ritual purpose

- Ritual clothing - optional, entirely depends on you being comfortable

If your ritual is conducted indoors, you may want to play relaxing music in the background.

Stage One

This is only a basic ritual, but you may prefer to use strongly energizing trees to mark the Directions. Choose the trees that resonate best with you and choose your own locations – what I tell you below is my personal choice and is just a guideline for you:

- **North – Earth – Hawthorn.** Hawthorn energy provides protection in the Circle and helps you to dispel any existing energy.
- **East – Air – Holly.** The holly is one of the guardian trees, great for empathy and balance.
- **South – Fire – Blackthorn.** This tree is for the magical power but if the energy proves too strong, try the hazel for divination and inspiration.
- **West – Water – Oak.** Another guardian tree, this one for growth and strength.

When you choose your trees, try to make sure that East/West and North/South have trees with similar energies. This helps balance the Circle, and if you want, you can even place a candle in each direction.

Stage Two

Now you need to set up your table or altar in the Circle, placing the big candle, your wands, focus object, and incense on it. Good wand options include:

- **Hazel –** Divination/inspiration meditations
- **Birch –** Cleansing, purity, and beginnings meditations
- **Hawthorn –** Protection workings or meditations
- **Rowan –** Cleansing/purity meditations
- **Ash –** Physical healing meditations

- **Willow** – Serenity, comfort, and harmony meditations

You can use up to three wands in the Circle but no more – this will depend on the meditation or working. This ritual uses just one. When you have all your objects on the table, light the incense and the candle. The room should be dark and quiet, and you can have soft music playing in the background.

Stage Three

Now you are ready for the ritual.

Start with the North direction and welcome the Earth element and the Hawthorn energy. As a mark of respect, you can recite the tree's properties. Then continue with directions sun-wise. Move to the East, the South, and the West, repeating the welcoming. You can touch the wands to connect physically with the trees and elements or use your ritual knife or Athame to point the directions.

Now your sacred Circle is done, and depending on what tradition you follow, you can acknowledge the Lord, Lady, God, or Goddess and welcome them to the Circle.

Note you need not start with North – you can start wherever suits you the best.

Stage Four

Seat yourself on a chair or the floor in front of your altar, facing whichever direction you want. Focus on what is on your table – the incense, candle, wands, and your focus object. If you want, you can beat on a drum rhythmically and gently, and when connected to and familiar with your objects, drink from the goblet or chalice. Feel the liquid going through your veins. At this stage, you may want to hold the hazel wand and use your favorite techniques for meditation to relax you. Breathe deeply and let yourself drift into a state of meditation. The hazel wand helps you enter a state of inspiration, divination, and wisdom. Stay like this for as long as you want.

Stage Five

When you have completed your meditation, dismantle your ritual. Starting in the West, thank the relevant element and tree energy and say farewell. Go anti-clockwise, to the South, East and North. When you have finished, put out the candle and the incense and take the objects from the table. The last thing to do is to remove the wands for the Four Directions.

If you want, you can leave everything where it is; although the ritual is done, the Circle will remain in place until you are ready to close it.

One of the more positive effects of working with tree energies and wands is that you gain more familiarity with the tree's spiritual energy when you walk among the trees in the forests, woods, and parks.

Chapter 10: The Druid Tarot

Images courtesy of https://horoscopes.lovetoknow.com/

Did the Druids even use tarot cards? That's the question many people ask, and answering it requires that you understand Pagan Tarot Decks are already a kind of "tradition." Two that spring to mind immediately are the Arthurian & Celtic Wisdom Tarots and the Merlin Tarot, and now we also have The Druidcraft Tarot.

The tarot is a tool to help you understand yourself and others and explore (and hopefully answer) metaphysical questions. It is also a tool for exploring and explaining spiritual systems, and that is why you sometimes see tarot decks that explore Alchemy or Zen as an example.

But it's been found that tarot is more than suitable for Paganism, which means it also suits Wicca and Druidry. That's because the Minor Arcana cards are based on the four elements, on their associations and powers. In contrast, the Major Arcana cards are based on awareness and understanding the dual forces - Ying/Yang, God/Goddess, Masculine/Feminine, etc.

But these aren't the only reasons Druidry and the tarot are linked. Classical authors say that the Druids taught Pythagorean Numerology, and we already know that numerology is the basis for traditional tarot. Bob Stewart, the Merlin Tarot author, suggested that we could find most of the Major Arcana card images in the Vita Merlini. It is more than possible that Ancient Bards used those images in their storytelling.

So, this is enough reason to create Druid tarot, but there is another, more compelling reason. Both Wicca and Druidry have a strong influence from the Golden Dawn, and most Druid tarot decks follow that theme through, building upon the inspiration from the Golden Dawn.

One of the more popular Druid tarot decks is the Druidcraft Tarot, accompanied by a book written by Phillip and Stephanie Carr-Gomm, both influential druids, and designed by Will Worthington.

Tarot card decks typically feature images that follow a specific theme, usually following one of two systems – Thoth or Rider-Waite-Smith. The Druidcraft deck is based on the Rider-Waite-Smith system and follows Druidry and Wicca themes.

All the Druid tarot decks are much larger than your average tarot deck, which measures around 8 ½ by 5 ½ inches. This does make them more difficult to handle if you are a beginner, but the more you handle them, the easier they become to shuffle and use.

The Simple Three-Card Draw

Simple three-card spreads work well if you have a yes-or-no question and is also suited to daily readings.

The Simple Three-Card Draw

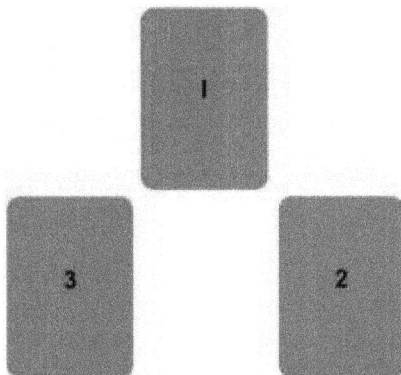

Method

1. Shuffle the tarot cards and cut them.

2. Take the top card from the bottom cut and place it in the card 1 position, facedown.

3. Put card 2 and card 3 face down in the positions you see above.

4. Turn the cards over, starting with 1, one at a time.

Yes-Or-No Readings

The person looking for advice or asking questions is known as the querent.

As the cards are being shuffled, cut, and then dealt out, the querent asks his or her question.

The first card is the answer and should be turned over from its side. If the card is upright, it's a yes, but if it is upside down, it is a no.

Cards 2 and 3 provide more information, explaining the yes-or-no answer.

- Card 2, on the right, details the motivation behind the question.

- Card 3, on the left, details future trends.

Daily Reading

When you do a daily reading, ask yourself a question – what you need to know for the day ahead or what you need to know about yourself on that day, for example.

- Card 1 indicates the superconscious mind and could be a message from on high.

- Card 2 is the asker (querent's) conscious and shows what they are bringing to the day.

- Card 3 is the asker (querent's) subconscious and indicates the subconscious programming – negative and positive – in play.

The Hexagram Spread

This spread is pretty flexible and comprises 7 cards, one of which is a significator. The hexagram is used for:

- Specific questions
- Daily readings
- Situation snapshots
- Guidance about a specific issue
- Advice

The Hexagram Spread

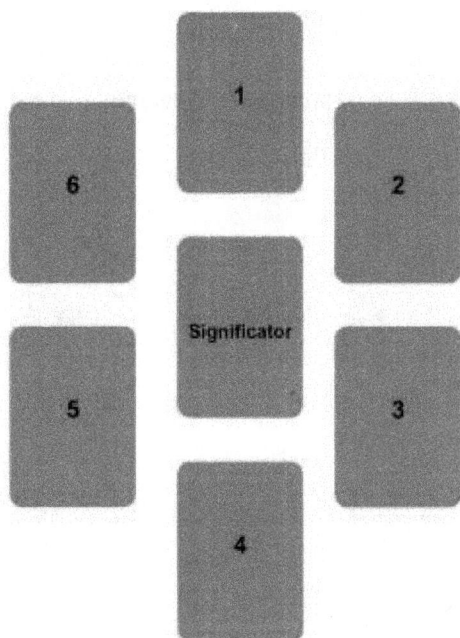

Method

1. Shuffle the cards and cut them.
2. Put the bottom cut on the top.
3. Deal the cards as above, face-up, using the first card from the bottom cut as the significator.
4. Starting from card 1, deal clockwise.

You can read this spread like a star with 6 points - the first, second, and sixth cards create an upwards triangle while the other three make a downwards triangle.

Interpretation

1. The significator card indicates an important thing about the querent.

2. The cards creating the upward triangle (1, 2, and 6) work as one, revealing the pros.

3. The cards creating the downward triangle (3, 4, and 5) also work as one, revealing the situation's downsides or cons.

The Major Arcana Quick Spread

As you would expect, only the major arcana cards are used in this spread, and it is only for answering critical questions or dealing with serious issues. There are 21 numbered cards and 1 unnumbered card (the Fool) in the major arcana.

The Major Arcana Spread

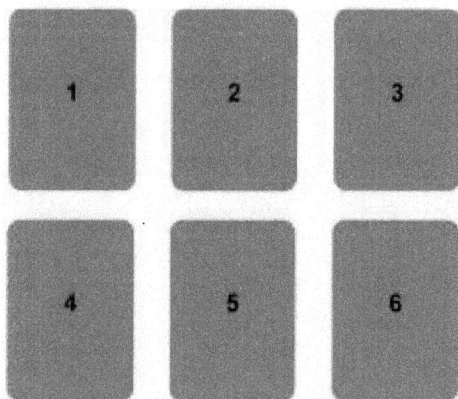

Method

1. Pull the major arcana cards from the deck.

2. Shuffle them and get the querent to cut them into three.

3. Turn all three piles face-up and take the top card from each pile. Place those cards, left to right, in a row.

4. Repeat, so you have two rows of cards.

Interpretation

• Cards 2 and 5 (the middle ones from each row) are important and answer the question or determine the outcome.

• The first, second, and third cards tell of things that will shortly happen.

• The fourth, fifth, and sixth cards tell of things that will happen later.

• The fourth card indicates helpful influences and benefits.

• The fifth and sixth cards indicate obstacles or something unexpected.

The Circular Spreads

Circular spreads are typically used for general yearly forecasts or zodiac spreads. Do take your time with these spreads as they have a lot of information to offer.

The Year Ahead Circular Spread

Each card focuses on one important issue for each month of the year ahead.

The Year Ahead Spread

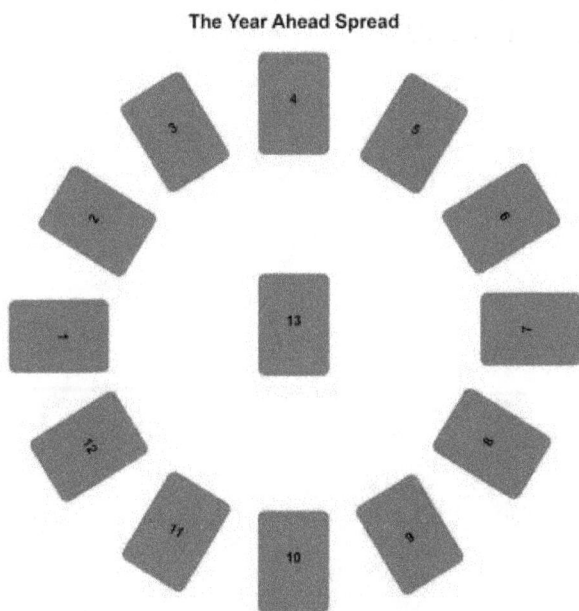

Method

1. The deck is shuffled twice, first by the reader and then by the querent.

2. The first card is placed face-up on the left (9 o'clock position).

3. The rest of the cards are dealt face-up, clockwise, with each one correspondent to a clock position.

4. A final card, the thirteenth, goes in the middle of the circle.

Interpretation

1. Begin with the middle card since this has an important message for the year.

2. The rest of the cards each represent one month, starting with card 1 as January.

3. Read the cards clockwise, beginning with the month of the reading.

4. Whether or not the cards are reversed, the interpretations are the upright meanings.

5. When each card is interpreted, the middle card should always be considered.

The Zodiac Circular Spread

In this spread, a card is placed in each astrological house. This is a good spread for giving guidance on specific life areas represented by the houses or for general readings.

The Zodiac Spread

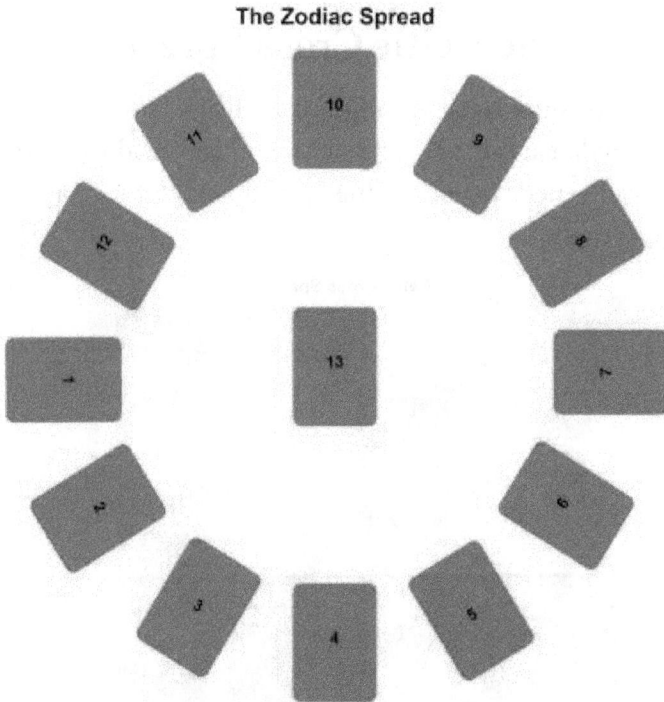

Method

1. The deck is shuffled by both, the reader first and the querent second.

2. The first card is placed face-up on the left (9 O'clock position).

3. The rest of the cards are dealt counter-clockwise and face-up.

4. The last card, 13, is placed in the center of the circle.

Interpretation

The 13th card indicates an important fact about the querent, while the remaining cards indicate matters relating to the house they are placed in. As with the previous spread, the 13th card must be remembered when all other cards are read.

The Celtic Cross Spread

This spread is the most common one. It uses the whole deck and is used for guidance on specific issues. You can read the cards one at a time, and the sheer beauty of the spread is that it tells a story, from the first card to the last.

Celtic Cross Spread

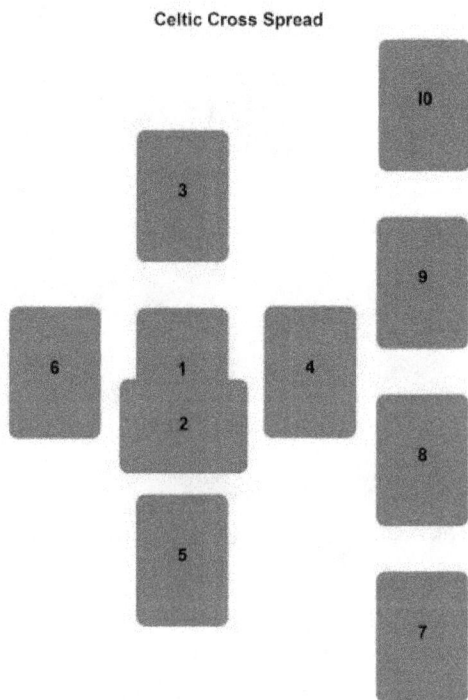

Method

1. First, select a significator that suits the querent and their question and place it face-up.

2. As the cards are shuffled, focus on the question.

3. The querent will then cut the cards with their right or left hand.

4. Put the cards in three piles, from left right, and facedown.

5. Pick the piles up, starting from the right and hold them in your palm, facedown, and start laying the spread out.

6. The first card goes on the significator.

7. The second is laid across the first, and the third goes beneath the significator.

8. The fourth goes to the left, while the fifth goes above the significator.

9. The sixth card goes to the right of the significator.

10. Using the remaining four cards, build a vertical line, starting from the bottom with the seventh card.

Interpretation

The Celtic Cross spread has ten positions:

1. Card 1 represents the present surrounding the querent's question.

2. Card 2 represents obstacles or influences relating to the question.

3. Card 3 represents any recent influences in the past that affect the question.

4. Card 4 represents previous events that the question is based on.

5. Card 5 represents the potential outcome or goal of the present position.

6. Card 6 represents the immediate influences in the future that affect the question.

7. Card 7 represents fears the querent may have.

8. Card 8 represents the opinions currently formed by the querent's friends and family.

9. Card 9 represents the querent's ideals and hopes.

10. Card 10 represents the results or answer to the question.

11.

Other Considerations

If the majority of the spread is major arcana cards, the querent has powerful influences at work in their life. Perhaps destiny will step in and take control of the result out of the querent's hands.

If any court card is in the first position, covering the significator, the rest of the cards must be read first. The situation must be assessed before considering whether the court card represents someone else, not the querent, or if you need to look for a different meaning.

If a court card is in the 10th position, a person of that coloring and age may decide the outcome.

Remember – although the cross has ten positions and each has its own meaning, they are all linked, and they all form a story.

When you interpret the tenth card, you must include everything from all the other cards.

If there is no conclusive outcome, you can lay another cross over the top, making sure you use card 10 as the significator.

The Pyramid Spread

The pyramid spread, containing 21 cards, is a two-part spread used for answering particular questions. Two pyramids are laid – an upright one, followed by an inverted one.

The Upright Pyramid

This pyramid summarizes the current situation for the querent.

The Pyramid Spread

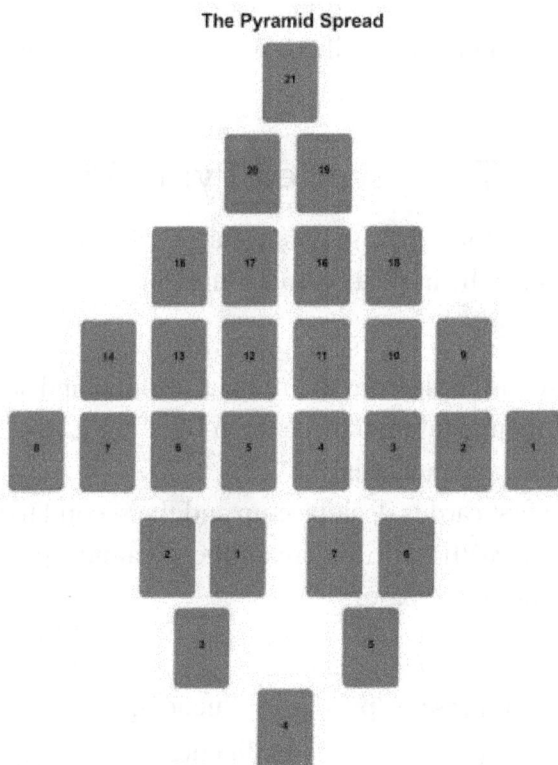

Method

    1. The cards are shuffled and cut as usual.

    2. All the cards are dealt facedown.

    3. The first eight cards are dealt in a left-to-right row.

    4. The next six cards are dealt right-to-left and centrally placed above the first row.

    5. Repeat until all 21 cards form an upright pyramid.

6. Turn cards 7, 14, and 21 over to gain an overview of the pyramid spread.

7. Then turn all cards over and interpret them as you would normally to get a general overview.

Interpretation

This pyramid provides an overview of the current situation for the querent. The bottom row of cards indicates past influences on the situation, while the most important card is the top one, 21, which represents any dominating influences. This card affects the whole reading.

The Inverted Pyramid

This spread is more precise in its answer to the question, but interpretation must be in relation to the upright pyramid's overview.

Method

1. Take the cards from the upright pyramid and shuffle them.
2. Cut them, and then place them back in the deck.
3. Shuffle and cut again.
4. The first card is dealt face-up and the second to the left.
5. The next three cards create the pyramid tip, and the final two cards finish the base.

Interpretation

- Card 1 represents previous influences.
- Card 2 represents current influences.
- Card 4 represents influences in the future.
- Card 5 represents the attitude of the people surrounding the querent.
- Card 6 represents obstacles.
- Card 7 represents the final outcome.

Conclusion

Has this book made you decide to change your life? Are you going to continue slogging along the same old path or choose a bright new future? If you haven't made up your mind just yet, I want you to do something for me.

Turn off your computer, your TV, your Kindle, or whatever you have on right now. Look out the window at the weather and change your clothes into something appropriate. Now get outside. Go for a walk. If you live in the city, head to the nearest park or drive to the nearest woods or countryside.

This walk will be different. Walk to somewhere quiet and peaceful, where you are alone. No matter where we walk, we take everything with us, all the baggage that accompanies us through life. We can't help but think about the bills that need paying, whether the car insurance is due, what's going to happen to a favorite character in a TV show, and so on. We focus on anything and everything, just not the walk, and it can sometimes feel as though you are carrying a voice with you, a voice that never shuts up, a voice that drowns out everything else.

We need those voices to pipe down, give us peace and quiet.

So, when you walk, find that quiet place in nature because you need to open your senses, and you can't do that with everything else going on around you.

When you get to your destination, raise your arms straight out to your sides. Look ahead of you, focus on a point just above the horizon, and then push back your arms just a little more. Start wiggling your fingers, and at the same time, begin to move your arms slowly forward until you can see your fingers at either side of you. Now stop. Continue to wiggle your fingers, but don't move your arms any further. Keep looking at that horizon. This is known as "seeing through the eyes of the owl."

Keeping your wiggling fingers in your peripheral view, slowly begin to lower your arms while remaining fully aware of everything around you. Stay in this position for a while.

Now bring your hands up to behind your ears and direct your hearing using your hands. Listen; think about how much you can hear. After a while, drop your hands and listen; focus deeply on what you can hear around you. I bet you can hear far more than you ever thought possible – all those sounds are always there, but you just don't hear them. Listen to everything- the sounds near you and those far away. This is known as "listening with the ears of the hare." Now, combine this with the eyes of the owl exercise.

Next, you want to work on your sense of smell. Reach to the ground and pick some grass. Scrunch it in your hands and smell it but not like you normally do. Typically, we smell something by sniffing in deeply, but this time, I want you to take short sniffs like a dog sniffs at a tree or the ground. Doing it this way allows you to smell much more than usual; try it with other things around you – a handful of earth, a twig, or leaves. This is known as "smelling through the nose of a fox." Now, sniff the air around you. At the same time, follow the owl and the hare exercises to bring all three senses together.

By now, you should already notice that the little voice has piped down. Once your awareness kicks into your physical senses, that voice can no longer compete, and it gradually disappears. Some people find it hard to focus on all three of these senses at the same time, so practice. Don't expect to get it right the first time. The more you practice, the better you will get at what we call standing meditation. Whenever you go for a walk, try to do these exercises, build up your relationship with the space that surrounds you. In time, it is easy to do, and you will become more in tune with nature.

It is the best place to start on your journey towards living a modern druid life.

Here's another book by Mari Silva that you might like

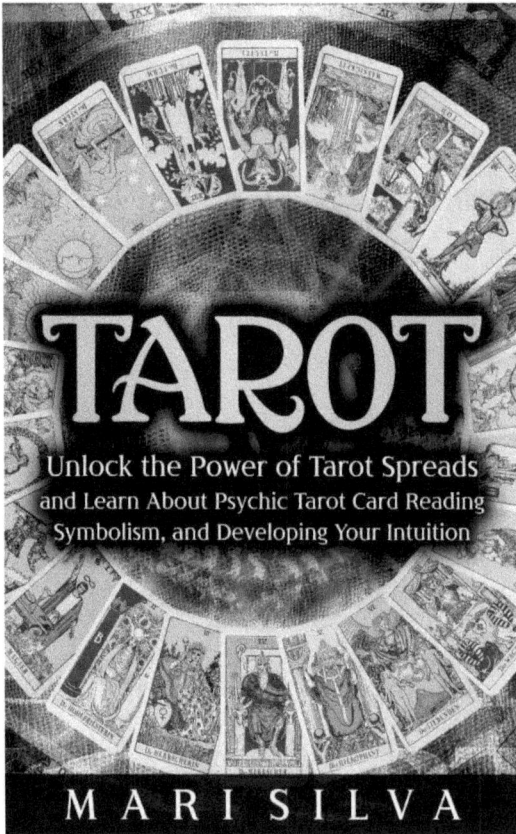

TAROT

Unlock the Power of Tarot Spreads and Learn About Psychic Tarot Card Reading Symbolism, and Developing Your Intuition

MARI SILVA

Your Free Gift (only available for a limited time)

Thanks for getting this book! If you want to learn more about various spirituality topics, then join Mari Silva's community and get a free guided meditation MP3 for awakening your third eye. This guided meditation mp3 is designed to open and strengthen ones third eye so you can experience a higher state of consciousness. Simply visit the link below the image to get started.

https://spiritualityspot.com/meditation

References

A Druid Meditation Primer – Ancient Order of Druids in America. (n.d.). Retrieved from https://aoda.org/publications/articles-on-druidry/druidmeditationprimer/

An Introduction to the Basics of Modern Druid Practice. (n.d.). The Druid Network. https://druidnetwork.org/what-is-druidry/learning-resources/shaping-the-wheel/introduction-basics-modern-druid-practice/

Carstairs, A. E. (2019, July 11). Ogham Divination. Divination Lessons. https://divinationlessons.wordpress.com/2019/07/11/ogham-divination/

Celebrations, Festivals and Holy Days. (n.d.). The Druid Network. https://druidnetwork.org/what-is-druidry/rites-and-rituals/rites-celebrate-seasonal-festivals/celebrations-festivals-holy-days/

Dana. (n.d.). daily divination. The Druid's Garden. Retrieved from https://druidgarden.wordpress.com/tag/daily-divination/

Druid Calendar | The Eightfold Wheel of the Year. (n.d.). Order of Bards, Ovates & Druids. https://druidry.org/druid-way/teaching-and-practice/druid-festivals/the-eightfold-wheel-of-the-year

Druid Prayer – A Druid Way. (n.d.). A Druid Way. Retrieved from https://adruidway.wordpress.com/category/druid-prayer/

druid ritual. (n.d.). The Druid's Garden. Retrieved from https://druidgarden.wordpress.com/tag/druid-ritual/

Druidry for Beginners - Where to Start? The Senses. (n.d.). Damh the Bard. Retrieved from https://www.paganmusic.co.uk/druidry-for-beginners-where-to-start-the-senses/

Ethics in Druidry | Druid Philosophy. (2019, November 27). Order of Bards, Ovates & Druids. https://druidry.org/druid-way/ethics-in-druidry

Gaia, Where Did the Ancient Druids Really Come From? (2019, August 30). Where Did the Ancient Druids Really Come From? | Gaia. Gaia. https://www.gaia.com/article/who-were-the-ancient-druids

Ghare, M. (2011, March 31). The Druidcraft Tarot Deck. Tarot-Ically Speaking. https://www.taroticallyspeaking.com/deck-review/the-druidcraft-tarot-deck/

Isabella. (2019, April 9). A Beginner's Understanding of Ogham Divination, Part One. Speaking of Witch Wands & Magickal Things. https://speakingofwitchwands.net/2019/04/09/a-beginners-understanding-of-ogham-divination-part-1/

Lesson Three ~ The Gods and Goddesses. (n.d.). The Druid Network. Retrieved from

https://druidnetwork.org/what-is-druidry/learning-resources/polytheist/lesson-three/

Lilly, J. (2008, August 14). Step By Step Magic: Simple Intention Manifestation. Druid Journal. https://druidjournal.net/2008/08/14/step-by-step-magic-simple-intention-manifestation/

Magical Skills in Druidic Ritual. (n.d.). ADF: Ár NDraíocht Féin: A Druid Fellowship. Retrieved from https://www.adf.org/rituals/explanations/magskills.html

Modern Druids | Neo Druids | Order of Bards, Ovates & Druids. (2020, October 22). Order of Bards, Ovates & Druids. https://druidry.org/druid-way/what-druidry/recent-history

Naming Rite. (n.d.). The Druid Network. Retrieved from https://druidnetwork.org/what-is-druidry/rites-and-rituals/rites-passage/naming-welcoming-rites/naming-rite/

Ogham alphabet. (n.d.). Omniglot.com. Retrieved from https://omniglot.com/writing/ogham.htm

Plant Lore | Druid Plant & Herb History | Order of Bards, Ovates & Druids. (2020, November 25). Order of Bards, Ovates & Druids. https://druidry.org/druid-way/teaching-and-practice/druid-plant-lore

The National Eisteddfod of Wales. (n.d.). Historic UK. Retrieved from https://www.historic-uk.com/HistoryUK/HistoryofWales/The-National-Eisteddfod-of-Wales/

What is Druidry ? | Order of Bards, Ovates & Druids. (2019, November 27). Order of Bards, Ovates & Druids. https://druidry.org/druid-way/what-druidry

Who were the Druids? (2019). Historic UK. https://www.historic-uk.com/HistoryUK/HistoryofWales/Druids/

www.ingramcontent.com/pod-product-compliance
Lightning Source LLC
Chambersburg PA
CBHW071859090426
42811CB00004B/664